Carrie M. Willard Among the Tlingits
The Letters of 1881-1883

Carrie M. Willard
Among the Tlingits
The Letters of 1881-1883

Carrie M. Willard Among the Tlingits: The Letters of 1881-1883

Published by Mountain Meadow Press
P.O. Box 318
Sitka, Alaska 99835

© 1995 by Mountain Meadow Press

Cover/Frontispiece Art by Nancy Behnken, Sitka, Alaska

First Edition
Printed on acid free paper in the United States of America

Main text distilled from LIFE IN ALASKA; LETTERS OF MRS. EUGENE S. WILLARD, edited by Mrs. Eva McClintock (Philadelphia: Presbyterian Board of Publication, 1883ca).

Willard, Eugene S., Mrs., 1853-1915.
   Carrie M. Willard among the Tlingits.
   p. cm.
   Includes bibliographical references and index.
   Preassigned LCCN: 95-75342
   ISBN 0-945519-20-6

   1. Willard, Eugene S., Mrs., 1853-1915--Correspondence. 2. Haines (Alaska)--History--19th century. 3. Chilkat Indians--Missions.   I. Title.

F914.H35255 1995   979.8'2
                                 QB195-227

Table of Contents

Illustrations

Acknowledgement

Several sketches that appear herein first appeared in historical publications other than LIFE IN ALASKA; LETTERS OF MRS. EUGENE S. WILLARD, 1883ca. Credits are noted under each of those sketches. Artists' names were not in most cases clearly visible nor otherwise credited in the publications in which the sketches first appeared. Mrs. Willard is known to have provided sketches for other authors, such as Dr. Sheldon Jackson, so that it is possible that some of the sketches that appear here from other publications were drawn by her. It is assumed that those of the sketches that appeared in LIFE IN ALASKA; LETTERS OF MRS. EUGENE S. WILLARD, 1883ca, were indeed drawn by Mrs. Willard, and thus for them, no bibiographic note is given.

Introduction

The story of America's *women of the frontier* has in the latter half of the twentieth century been increasingly finding its way into print—focusing on the women themselves as historically significant players in the development of the frontier.

The story of Carrie M. Willard's life among the Tlingits focuses on the frontierswoman, even though she was a woman *at the side of* a man. Her husband Eugene had been granted the title "missionary," but, as is evident in her letters, Carrie could have borne the same title, for her role among the Tlingits equaled his in most respects. Surely, too, those qualities of character which enabled Eugene Willard to venture into nineteenth century Southeast Alaska were equally possessed by the woman who accompanied him.

We should thus recognize that, despite the call to service, Christian women setting out on their own for Alaska or, like Carrie, traveling alongside missionary husbands, personified more than religious zeal. Their recorded experiences demonstrate that they were adventurous, self-assured, determined, and courageous. They were entering relatively unknown regions and would live among groups of people considered *hostiles*. These women knew they could at any time be called upon to fend for themselves, to face serious illness or the loss of children, to suffer food shortages, and to encounter life-threatening dangers.

These frontierswomen realized they would not see their families and friends back home for months or years, only communicating infrequently by letter. These women knew they would leave behind all cultural and social familiarities and the fashions and conveniences to which they were accustomed.

We must look, too, at the story of Carrie M. Willard as part of a larger historical panorama. The broadest canvas, of course, spans the entire sweep of European culture across the North American continent, which began with early seventeenth century colonization on the East Coast. During the seventeenth and eighteenth centuries, missionaries wound like the continent's rivers first throughout the eastern regions and then branching into the Midwest. During the nineteenth century, missionaries of varying denominations extended their reaches further westward, seeking, as they put it, "new flocks."

With the United States' purchase of Alaska from the Russians in 1867, American missionaries set sights on this newest of frontiers. The Presbyterians surveyed potential Native populations and selected Southeast Alaska's Tlingit Indians as worthy of missionary efforts. The Presbyterians began sending representatives of the church to the region in the late 1870s.

In a report to the Presbyterian Board of Home Missions prior to the assignment of Carrie Willard and her husband Eugene to their work among the Tlingits, the Rev. A. L. Lindsley discussed the earliest existing missionary operations in Southeast Alaska, which he had visited. In his report, we see the groundwork that led to the arrival of the

Willards in Alaska and meet several of the people mentioned in Carrie's letters. He wrote:

Sitka and Fort Wrangell are the only points at which schools have been established. At the former, our school was suspended in consequence of the removal of Miss Kellogg to Fort Wrangell, on her marriage with our missionary there, Rev. S. Hall Young. Rev. John G. Brady, who was appointed as missionary to Sitka, resigned after a few months' trial.

At Fort Wrangell, the missionary in charge is Rev. Young. He arrived there in August, 1878. Mrs. A. R. McFarland is mistress of the Industrial School for girls. She arrived in 1877. Miss M.J. Dunbar, teacher in day-school, arrived in 1879. These are all under the appointment of our Board of Home Missions. Rev. W. R. Corlies, M.D., and his wife arrived in 1879. They are Baptists. Dr. Corlies has begun the practice of medicine, and Mrs. Corlies is engaged in teaching Indian children. Two day-schools, therefore, beside the Industrial School, are in operation at Fort Wrangell.

...over all that broad region [Southeast Alaska] no regular effort to evangelize the natives has ever been made until very recently... The work of evangelizing these people seems to have been allotted to us in a remarkable manner.

After comparison of facts and opinions, the writer advocates the restriction of our Alaskan missions to the Tlingit people...

A powerful sub-tribe, the "Chilkats," numbering one thousand, occupies the area around Lynn Canal and Chilkat River... I talked with Chief Kakee and a band of Chilkats. Rev. S. Hall Young was present to assist. We confirmed our impressions that the Chilkats were accessible to Christian influences and desired the introduction of school and teachers.

The Chilkats are connected by ties of kindred with the Stickeens of Wrangell, and although the distance by canoe is between two and three hundred miles, the former often visit the latter, and many Chilkats come to Fort Wrangell, as do various other Tlingits, for trade. Though their country is remote from the course of ships and is the most distant and farthest inland of the remarkable district under our survey, the Chilkats' constitutional vigor, intellectual traits, and independent spirit give them a commanding position among the tribes and qualify them for great usefulness after they shall have received the Gospel.

In some respects, the Chilkat mission will be more important than the Sitka mission, for the Chilkat mission will open the way to the interior...and beyond the Chilkat River...

With Rev. Young at Wrangell, another at Sitka, and a third at Lynn Canal among the Chilkats, intelligence could be conveyed along lines of the triangle, harmony and cooperation could be maintained, and influence and efforts could be united as occasion might require.

In an update report on Southeast Alaska submitted to the Board of Home Missions, May 1, 1881, the chairperson of the board's Executive Committee, E. M. Condit, wrote,

In the Fall of 1879, Mr. [S. Hall] Young visited the tribes in the northern part of the archipelago and recommended that the Chilkats...be supplied with a missionary as soon as possible. The Home Board has shown its confidence in his judgment by adopting his recommendations in each case. A missionary was commissioned for Chilkat in the summer of 1880, but was diverted to another field. In June of that year Mr. Young...sent to that tribe as missionary teacher Mrs. Sarah Dickinson, a native of the...[Tsimpsian] tribe—speaking the same language...The Board confirmed her commission, and she has been laboring very successfully ever since—the Chilcats welcoming her warmly and continuing to send their children to her school.

Last August, Mr. Young again visited these Northern tribes, spending some time among the Chilkats. He carefully studied the condition of each of the four villages of that tribe and selected a point on a beautiful harbor accessible to all, upon good farming land and where the Northwest Trading Company has its post, as the site for a mission and a new Indian town. He selected a site for a church and made arrangements with the Company, who had the lumber on the ground, to build a comfortable house for church and school. The head men of all these villages pledged themselves to obey the coming missionary, to build a new town of 'white man's houses,' and to support the school. Thus the mission has long been located, and all is in readiness for the missionary. Rev. Eugene S. Willard, who goes up by the June steamer with his wife and daughter to take charge of that mission, will find a people eagerly expecting him, and an open door for the entrance of Christian civilization.

The situating of "a new Indian town" usually was essential to missionary work among nineteenth century Indian groups, who were traditionally at least semi-nomadic for seasonal hunting and gathering. The missionaries did not wish to trek with the Indians to fish camps, caribou routes, edible plant sites, and so on, in order to preach. They wanted the Indians to come to an established mission location and to stay there most of the time. Where mission land was arable, the missionaries and their wives taught agricultural skills and encouraged the Natives to grow domestic foods for themselves. In parts of Southeast Alaska this is only marginally possible, but the Willards did garden and engage Native children in garden work, and the women and girls in produce processing.

In other words, the *work* involved more than the teaching of Christian doctrine by "the missionary." It involved education in the broader sense, domestication of the common American sort, the continual application of Christian principles to daily-life situations, and doctoring, all of which most often fell to Carrie.

Thus, launching into the letters, the reader may anticipate witnessing, in a most unusual setting, the life of an extraordinary woman.

Borg Hendrickson
Sitka, Alaska

Editorial Note

Caroline McCoy White was born in New Castle, Pennsylvania, May 3, 1853. Early in life "Carrie" became fascinated with the lives of Christian missionaries about whom she heard and read, even to the point of founding a missionary society of little girls. Her education as a child was limited due to prolonged illness, but included reading, home-schooling, and art instruction. As a young adult she studied art at academies in Cincinnati, New York City, and Pittsburgh and taught drawing and painting at United Presbyterian College, Monmouth, Illinois. Many of the sketches that appear in this present volume were originally drawn by Carrie.

She became Mrs. Eugene Willard on April 24, 1879. That summer, she and her husband accepted Southeast Alaska mission positions under the auspices of the Presbyterian Board of Home Missions. In the early summer of 1881, the Willards, with toddler daughter Carrie, arrived in Alaska, and it was then that Mrs. Willard began writing the letters that comprise this text. As they appear here, the letters have been edited primarily to simplify syntax, modernize English spellings, eliminate repetitions, and to objectify overtly one-sided representations of Tlingit Indian customs. Spellings and interpretations of Tlingit words herein are those of Carrie Willard and, thus, may not coincide with today's Tlingit language. To aid identification of people mentioned in the letters, an annotated biographical list appears at the back of the book.

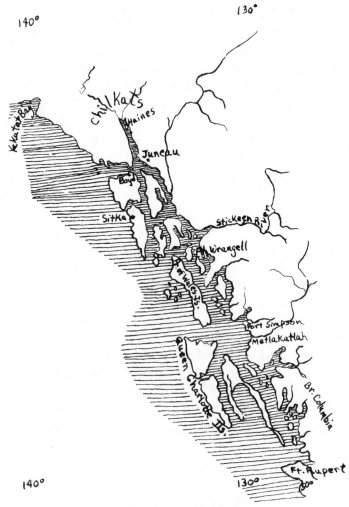

140°

130°

chillkats

Haines

K.Vutaz Bay

Juneau

Bay

Sitka

Stickeen R.

Wrangell

Bwells Is.

Port Simpson

Metlakatlah

Queen Charlotte Ids.

Br. Columbia

140°

130°

Ft. Rupert

50°

Southeast Alaska
(facsimile of Carrie M. Willard map)

Carrie M. Willard
Among the Tlingits
The Letters of 1881-1883

MRS. EUGENE WILLARD
SHELDON JACKSON INSTITUTE
SITKA, ALASKA
JUNE 21, 1881

MY DEAR PARENTS: You will be surprised that we are still in this place, when by our last letter you heard that we were to sail in a few days for Chilkat, and it is difficult for the moment to go back and see things as you see them and know exactly *what* to tell you, when so much more than is possible to tell in this slow way comes crowding upon the mind. We were under orders to stop either at Fort Wrangell or Sitka for a month; so we came on to Sitka, and were brought to the home of Mr. Alonzo E. Austin and his family, who are in charge of the mission here. We have found them devoted and worthy people, who warmly took us to their hearts and home.

On Friday last the steam-launch of the United States ship *Jamestown* returned from the mines with the word that there was war in Chilkat; that

1

two men had been killed and several wounded, all on one side; that fighting would go on till both sides were even; that the *Favorite* would bring further word, and, if necessary, a squad of United States Marines would be detached for duty there.

The *Favorite* came in on Monday with word that the fighting was still hot. Commander Henry Glass, of the *U.S.S. Jamestown*, waited on us to say that we could not possibly accomplish anything by going up there now. Wanting no more complications, he much desired to have us wait here until Dr. Sheldon Jackson should arrive.

This morning the soldiers left for Chilkat. The head chief was away at the beginning of the trouble, and it is said that he expresses himself as so grieved and disgusted that he wishes to come to Sitka until the trouble is settled, lest Captain Glass should hold him responsible. The Indians here expressed great sorrow about the fighting. We are waiting for Dr. Jackson, by the next steamer, who will bring with him the lumber and materials for our building. In the meantime, our hearts and hands are full and we are praying.

Mr. Willard preached to the whites Sabbath last. Yesterday he helped put in potatoes for the boys' school which Mr. Austin has started. Mr. Willard made a nice bedstead and expects to make a number of things in the way of furniture before we start. As there is no minister here, he will fill the place while we remain.

JUNE 24

Mr. Willard officiated at the funeral of the wife of Chief Anahootz this morning, as the chief consented to have a Christian burial. It was a sad death. Captain Glass had forbidden the making or selling of hoochinoo [liquor] and appointed this chief and several other Indians as policemen, and, as a result, the town is more orderly. But on last Sabbath several Indians clubbed together and bought a gallon of alcohol and drank until this one of the party died. Her body was carried home amid great excitement. The Indians hold the one whom they detailed to carry the whiskey to them responsible for the death and will not tell who sold the stuff except that it was a white man.

It is the custom of the Indians to compel the person responsible to stay beside the corpse until it is finally disposed of. Then, in a council, they decide how many "blankets" he shall pay. If he fails to pay the price, he may be killed. Captain Glass heard the case Monday and allowed them to carry out their custom so far as having the accused, Indian Charley, stay with the corpse, but said that he, Captain Glass, would decide what penalty should be paid. This morning Charley heard that the Indians were going to ask a great many blankets—more than he could possibly pay—and said that he would kill himself rather than be arrested. He is a large, powerful man; so, to save him from himself and from his people, the captain sent him to the guard-house, and there they put him in irons. We do not know what is to be done.

The captain sent for Mr. Willard to attend the "pow-wow" (council) on Monday, and afterward asked him to attend to the funeral service. The captain and his officers were in attendance, and other whites. The funeral was held in the house of Anahootz. Hymns were sung; then Mr. Willard spoke of death—what it is—the judgment, the individual accountability of each soul for deeds done in the body. Mr. Austin followed.

Then the friends took leave of the body, after which it was carried out through an opening made by the removal of some boards from the side of the house, as the Tlingits have a superstition against taking a corpse through the usual door of a house. They led out a dog before the coffin—so that it may receive the thrusts of the evil spirits that beset the way and thereby prevent sickness from coming into the house.

We have had no recent word from the Chilkat country—none since the *Favorite* left. She is not expected back before the mail steamer *California* leaves Sitka.

SHELDON JACKSON INSTITUTE
SITKA, ALASKA
JUNE 29, 1881

MY DEAR FRIENDS: For many days I have wished for the opportunity of writing you something of the good work in this land. The opportunity comes this morning while Baby sleeps, and now I realize how difficult it is to select from so large a collection just the facts that will be the most interesting and convey to you the truest impressions. This is a wonderful country in many respects. During the summer months it is literally a land where there is no night. The sun sinks below the mountaintop at about nine p.m. I sat sewing last night till near eleven, then retired by daylight. We have dusk only for about one hour at midnight, and then the broad day streams in again. One could read all night without a lamp. We are so near the north pole that at this season but little of the sun's circuit is invisible. It rises, I think, at about one-sixth of the circle from its setting. I believe that from the height of Mount Saint Elias we could see the sun's course around the horizon without a moment's shadow. In winter here, we are told, the days are correspondingly short: sunset at two or three in the afternoon.

The mountains which enclose this picturesque village are white with snow, while on the table at my side stands a bowl of the most beautiful berries I ever saw—the salmonberries, which are apparently a cross of the strawberry, which they resemble in color and form, and the blackberry, which they are more like in seed, cells and flavor. In the last particular, all fruits that I have eaten here are inferior, having a peculiar wild, woody taste; but I believe that by culture much better varieties could be obtained.

Since writing this I have eaten salmonberries which are as large as crabapples and very delicious. In appearance they are certainly all that could be desired. We had lettuce, too, from the garden here, yesterday—very nice—and radishes, peas, cauliflowers, cabbage, potatoes and turnips; and many other things growing beautifully.

We stopped but two hours in Fort Wrangell on the way here. There was so much to be seen and heard. The town of Wrangell is a mud-hole and a wharf; at least, it must have been only that before the missionaries made it a home also. Subtract

Indian Village at Fort Wrangell
(from J.D. Cox *Letter of the Secretary of the Interior*)

the [McFarland Mission] Home and the little signs of life through the town which are clearly the Home's emanations, and Wrangell is a scene of desolation such as would fill your hearts with a new appreciation of the spirit which sustained Mrs. McFarland when the steamer left her the only white woman in the place. She is the general, and Miss Maggie J. Dunbar is her under-officer.

The Home is a large and plain but substantial building with double porch to the front, looking out over the lovely harbor and its green islands, locked in by the snow-capped mountains which almost crowd the little town into the water. The twenty-eight girls were grouped on the upper porch and made a sweet picture in the light of the setting sun—a picture the details of which grew upon us as we mingled among them. After we

At McFarland Home, Fort Wrangell
(from S. Jackson, *Alaska*)

Rev. Corlies, Wife & Boy   Mrs. McFarland & Girls   Rev. Young, Wife
Miss Dunbar   Mrs. Dickinson

saw the house, which is surprisingly complete in
its appointments, the bathroom (with ready
faucets) outside the dormitory, the bake house,
wash houses, the girl's sitting room, and the sick
room—which, happily, was unoccupied, the girls
were called into the school room to sing for us.

I am sure that no one could have heard their
sweet voices without wishing to have a share in
this work. The children looked so proud and
happy! They are quick and bright. The Home is
an industrial school—the housework, sewing and
everything done by classes in turn.

With them on this trip, Mr. [and Mrs. S. Hall]
Young had the Hydah girl of about ten years whom
they had adopted from the Home. I was sketching
on deck one day, and she became inspired. She sat

7

Presbyterian Church & McFarland Home, Fort Wrangell

in perfect rapture looking at the mountains, sky and water. At one point of particular beauty she exclaimed, with her hands on her breast and her face all aglow, "Oh, my heart gave a great shake!" At another place Mrs. Young told her to sketch the scene at sunset. She sat with a countenance worthy a great artist. Gazing over the shining deep with softened eyes, she simply said, "I can't draw glory." This child's father, now dead, was the finest artist and silversmith on the coast. Beautiful work in carving and weaving is still done.

The Indian women, by the way, sew beautifully. After we came up here to Sitka, I gave my Stickeen girl, Kittie (whom I brought with me from the McFarland Home), some handkerchiefs to hem, some with the portraits of our President and Vice President, which I intended as presents to the Chilkat chiefs, and I know that few white girls at her age would have done the work so well. I also cut out a new dress for her, and she made the skirt very nicely. By the last steamer she sent to "Dear Mrs. McFarland" a letter which I wish you could have seen, written in a plain hand, in simple yet dignified language, with not a word misspelled except my name.

There were flowers about the house. Between the McFarland Home and the church building was a garden. On the other side of the church stood the cottage of those consecrated missionaries Dr. W. H. R. Corlies and wife. They came in June, 1879, from Philadelphia with their one boy of eight or ten years. They have now a dear baby girl. These, with the Rev. S. Hall Young and wife, make up the mission force at Wrangell, where is the only organized evangelical church in Alaska.

Here in Sitka great work has been done and is going on. In looking over the field I am impressed with two things—the wonderful results already accomplished and the infinitely greater work yet to be done. It is word by word and word upon word; it is in some sense like the work of the blacksmith, under whose hammer the iron constantly cools. Over and over again it must go to the forge, and the hammer must know no rest.

Rev. John G. Brady was the first gentleman sent out by a Board to Alaska. He came to Sitka in the spring of 1878. Sometime after, Miss Kellogg joined him as the teacher of the school and had not been here more than six months when she went to Wrangell as the wife of Rev. Mr. Young. Soon after, Mr. Brady resigned the charge of the mission. Mr. Alonzo E. Austin, a friend of Mr. Brady's in New York, came here for his health, and after the breaking up of the mission, opened a school for the Russian children, which he carried on till the arrival of his family about a year ago. Then the school was transferred to the hands of his second daughter, the elder daughter having brought with her a commission as teacher to the Indians. Rev. G.W. Lyons and wife were then sent as missionaries to this station. They stayed but a year, when, on account of ill health, they were obliged to return to California. Soon after, Mr. Austin received a teacher's commission also, he and his daughter being the force here at present.

During our stay, my husband preaches in the custom-house on the Sabbath, and we have prayer meeting Wednesday evenings. Mr. Austin seems to be abundantly qualified for the work here, and I hope he will be ordained and given charge of this station. He has a power really remarkable in adapting himself, his thoughts and his words to the condition of the Indians. They seem to like him very much, and he and his daughter have inaugurated a work which already has done much good and promises so much more.

This leads me to speak of the Boys' Home at Sitka, which is only started and numbers twenty-three boys, with others pleading to be taken in. But until the support of some of the scholars is guaranteed by friends in the East, Mr. Austin fears to incur more debt; so the little fellows are turned away. It was in this way the Home originated: Some of the boys attending the day-school begged to stay in the building overnight. They were at length taken in, and others pleaded for the same privilege. So the Home began and was named by the missionaries "Sheldon Jackson Institute" after Dr. Jackson, who was not only the first American minister to visit this section in the interests of missions, but has also become the "father of Alaska missions" by his success in securing missionaries and funds for the work.

You must hear of the work of Captain Henry Glass, of the *U.S.S. Jamestown*, stationed here the past two or three years. Not often does the government send out a missionary, but they have in this young commander. His first move was to make it a crime to sell, buy or drink any intoxicating drinks. He prevailed upon the traders to sell no molasses in quantities, so that no one could make drink. He issued orders in regard to the cleaning up of the ranche (the Indian quarters). He appointed a police force of Indian men, in navy-cloth, with "Jamestown" in large gilt letters on their caps and a silver star on their breasts.

He made education compulsory in this way: The houses were all numbered, and the children of each house. Each child was given a little round tin plate on which was marked his or her number, thus: "House No. 17, Boy No. 5." These plates were worn on a string about the neck. As soon as the children came into school, they were registered. Whoever failed to send their children to school was fined a blanket. When the Indians discovered that the captain was in earnest, they submitted. Now, if any are going off on a fishing tour, the head of the house comes and explains why his children will be absent and for how long. In this way the school attendance has been doubled, the highest being two hundred and seventy-one; this is the mission day-school.

Most of the women are clothed right neatly in calico dresses, which they make themselves and keep very clean. Universal outside garments,

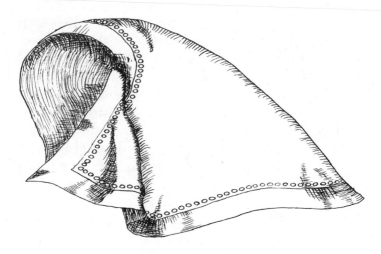

Tlingit Button Blanket

their blanksts are as white as snow, those that are not dyed. Some of the latter are very handsome. I have seen several of a beautiful navy blue with a stripe of crimson, on each side of which was a close scale-row of pearl buttons; the stripe passed round the neck and down the front. An orange-colored silk handkerchief on the head and a pair of light-colored moccasins complete the outfit. Their blankets are worn with grace, a party of Indians making a picturesque group. They all wear jewelry and prefer silver to gold. Some of the women wear as many as a dozen pairs of bracelets at once. These are made of coin beaten out and beautifully engraved. They cost from a dollar and a half per pair to five dollars, the price varying according to width and weight.

The ranche has been cleaned, whitewashed and drained. Some pleasant new houses are being put up. All is peaceful and quiet where a few

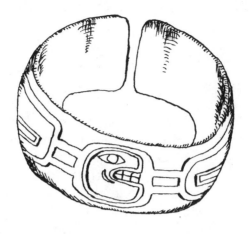

Tlingit Bracelet Made of Silver

months ago it was a place of strife. But the work did not stop there: the whole town has been renovated. Streets have been cleaned, trees planted, a sea wall built, the common made tidy, etc.

The boys who are staying at the school had boarded themselves, but now a room has been fixed up a little for them. They have a tin box lid tacked up as a looking glass. This is in the old barracks building where the Austins are living. Captain Glass had the school removed to another government building, quite large and in a beautiful location down the beach. An effort is being made now to secure it for the mission, which has been promised the free use of it as long as they occupy it. There is a large garden attached, from which, it is hoped, they will have a considerable income over and above supplying the Home with vegetables. The captain had the building whitewashed and fixed up generally—had the ship's carpenter make the bunks for the boys, and benches, tables, etc. In fact, he has seemed to turn the crew into a mission force. He and his young wife at the head work with their own hands and encourage in every way the earnest and devoted teachers. So now this staying overnight of a few boys has developed into a boys' boarding and industrial school. The boys do their own work, even sewing now, under the ship's tailor, on a second suit of clothes for themselves of cotton-jean. They and the outside children attend school together in the morning, and on Sabbath morning, service is held in the school room there.

I could not keep back the tears of joy when I attended their meeting and saw these children, listening with bright, eager faces to the tidings which have gladdened so many hearts and in their turn repeating in unison the Ten Commandments and the beautiful assurances of God's love. Then, with sweetly solemn voices, hands clasped and heads bowed, they prayed together. I never before heard the Lord's Prayer repeated to beautifully. And still there is so much to do; only a beginning has been made. The great house, after all, is very barren, cold and damp, and the boys do not have bedclothes to keep them warm. They, so far, have found blankets, but these are insufficient, and one little fellow has none. The weather never gets warm here. We have fire every day and sleep under clothing almost as heavy as in winter at home; so that, at least before winter comes, these boys ought to have some comfortables.

Another opportunity for kind hearts and willing hands is the sick room in the Home. It is a dark, bleak room containing only two cots and a stool or two—no warm comforts, not even a rug for the floor and without curtains for the windows and pictures for bare walls. In the school there is a little fellow named Lawrence, who has an abscess, and the doctor says that he cannot live more than two years. Soon, I fear, Lawrence will be confined to this miserable room. How nice it would be if some of those who have beautiful rooms at home could spare something to beautify this! He is a bright, sweet-faced, patient boy, and Mr. Austin says he has just to pull him back from work, although the boy is so thin and weak.

The school room is pleasant. Miss Austin and I colored Bible scenes for the walls, which with ceiling, were painted white with a blue cornice. Mrs. Beardslee presented blue calico, which we made into curtains. In this room is the organ, and they expect to furnish the windows with plants.

Another thing I meant to speak of: The Indians, and particularly our tribe, do beautiful work carving spoons and forks of wood and bone, and weaving baskets, table mats, hats, etc., from the inner bark of trees. Besides pretty, these are durable, and we wish to encourage every industry among them and develop every talent. I intend to design some things for them after awhile and to offer rewards for designing among themselves. We would like to have an outlet for this work.

I have not spoken of the language. It is difficult, but the Sitka, Stickeen and Chilkat tribes speak the same. I have been studying with Kittie and have quite a number of words; but oh, it is so hard to be tongue-tied when the heart is full!

Chilkat Baskets and Horn Spoon

We expect Dr. Jackson by the *California* next week, after which we hope to have a party with us to Chilkat; so that the next letter will tell you of a field which heretofore has been unoccupied by any mission.

And now, with loving remembrances and prayer for mutual blessings in this great work, I am

Truly your friend,
Carrie M. Willard

Carved Implements
1,2. Chilkat rattles. 3. Wooden bowl.
4. Wooden pipe. 5. Wooden comb.

SITKA, ALASKA
JULY 8

Chilkat is some two hundred and twenty-five miles north of this place, through Chatham Straits. The steamer leaves in forty-eight hours, and we go with her as far as the mines. Dr. Sheldon Jackson is aboard, with carpenters and lumber for the building of the mission house, which we hope to occupy before long...

17

MY DEAR FRIENDS: In the beginning, a word to friends old and young who had part or parcel in the sending of the singing books which arrived last evening by the man-of-war *Wachusette*. How we do thank you all for your prompt kindness! We feel so strong—that is, your ready action in this matter has made us feel that we have your interest, your love and your prayers. And, as we said to each other when we opened the books last night, "Oh, how good it will seem to sing from books that our home friends have sent!" It seems good even to have them in the house.

And now where shall I begin to tell you of all you wish to know of our work? You know we expected to live in a tent till we could put up for ourselves a log house. Well, we should have done so had it not been for Dr. Sheldon Jackson's wise and unselfish zeal. Instead of waiting until someone proffered the means, he had faith in the loving interest of the Church at large to redeem the pledge he might make and borrowed money on his own responsibility to erect buildings for the mission both here and at Hoonah. Then, as the mere mechanical part of building was no simple problem so far from supplies, he brought his own experience to bear upon it, and with his carpenters worked with his own hands on our pretty home here. He also brought us a bell—the gift of Mrs. C.H. Langdon of Elizabeth, New Jersey—which is the first Presbyterian bell in Alaska; and oh how sweet it sounds. Just a perfect Presbyterian tone!

Mission at Haines, Alaska

I can never express the feelings it aroused when I first heard the waves of its solemn music in the solitude of Alaska. It is such a help to us! Twice every Sabbath it brings the Natives together to hear the good news, and on every weekday to a school. Dr. Jackson expects, on his return to the States, to solicit funds to pay for our building.

And now as to our field and work here. I shall give you an idea of it. You have heard of the British mission under the care of Father Duncan, who has built the model Christian Indian village of Metlakatlah in British Columbia. It is with something of the same plan in mind that we have located our mission on Portage Bay, where there is no permanent Indian house. We have named our mission after the secretary of the Woman's Executive Committee of Home Missions, "Haines."

19

In our Chilkat country there are four villages—three on Chilkat River and one on the Chilkoot River. Each of these villages has its chief or chiefs and medicine men, each its distinct nobility, and each its own interests and jealousies of all the others. So, you see, had we built at any one of these places, we would in some measure come into antagonism with the others. We would, in their eyes, be allying ourselves with that particular people, and the others would be too proud to come under their hand. As it is, Portage Bay is a beautiful and safe harbor almost at the head of Chilkoot Inlet, the eastern arm of Lynn Canal. The point of land here between the Chilkat River and Lynn Canal is the largest level tract and the most fertile that we have seen anywhere in Alaska, and will afford ample farming ground for the people. They all regard it as our place and so speak of it and have promised in all the villages to come to "the minister's place" and build new houses where they can learn. They have visited us, and one and all have expressed their joy at our arrival and their own intention to come and build here as soon as the winter stores of fish and berries are secured.

Besides our own house here, there are buildings put up by the trading company, one occupied by them as a trading post, the other purchased by the Mission Board for school purposes. The school is sixteen by thirty feet, of rough and knotty up-and-down boards, without chimneys, with four small windows which cannot be opened, and one small door. The door is so frail that I fear it will scarcely stand a good winter storm, for it shakes with walking down the steps. The rafters above have been covered with whitewashed cheescloth, which flaps up and down like a sail every time the door is opened. There are so many holes in the shingles that on a sunshiny day this whited canopy presents the appearance of the starry heavens, so flecked with sunlight. It will perhaps do for a year or two.

The company's store is kept by their agent, George Dickinson, an American whose wife is a Tsimpsian Indian woman who went to school to Father Duncan and was converted by him. It was she who was working in a little school of her own in Wrangell when, in 1877, Dr. Jackson and Mrs. McFarland went there. After their arrival she acted as interpreter, until, just a year ago, her husband was sent here by the company, and she was commissioned by the Board to open a school for the Chilkats. She is a very good woman and has done well under the circumstances. We shall soon need a teacher of larger scope, but Mrs. Dickinson is retained for the present as teacher under Mr. Willard, and as an interpreter.

We opened the school on Monday, the 8th of August, after Dr. Jackson left, with twenty-four pupils. Some days since we have had twenty-eight, but only four regular ones. The others came in as they crossed the trail. There are a few bark shelters, where they stop when they come to trade. But on every Sabbath canoe-loads come from the villages, and we have always had from forty-five to fifty in attendance. Monday five other canoes came in for church. Their having missed a day, we taught them in our home. These are principally from Chilkoot and the lower villages. The others are too far away, and the people too busy, except in the uppermost, where they have been hindered by war. We have now their promises of peace and that the people will come down soon. We are hoping to commence regular work by the first of October. Although we have scarcely breathing time now, we hope to visit all the villages before that time.

We have already made the trip to Chilkoot, and I must tell you about it. The chief, Don-a-wok, of the lower village, has a large canoe, and one day he sent a messenger up to ask us to go out with him on the bay. We gladly consented, and at sunset we pushed off with eight paddles. We had a delightful time singing some gospel hymns at the chief's request. He offered also the service of his boat to take us to Chilkoot. So the next day I spent in preparing lunch for the party, and on the second morning, bright and early, we set sail and dipped paddle for Chilkoot, thirty-two souls comfortably seated, and still room for as many more. Putting into a bay below the rapids, we left the boat and took the trail to the village, about a mile distant, which we reached about noon. We found the news of our coming had preceded us long enough for the chiefs to have everything in readiness. We were conducted to the house of the head chief, who is also a medicine man, and were received with the greatest kindness.

The house was exceedingly neat, the hard, burnished floor boards being white and clean. Sand was sprinkled over the fireplace in the center. We mounted the high steps outside to a low,

Tlingit House Front
(from A. Krause, *Die Tlingit Indianer*)

arched doorway. Passing through, we found ourselves on a little platform from which two or
three steps led down to a second platform of
greater breadth and extending around the entire
building. Two or three feet from its edge hung
tent cloth, curtaining in sleeping and storage
rooms on the sides. The far end of the room, back
of the fireplace, is the seat of honor. In this case it
consisted of chests covered with white muslin.
Back of it, arranged on a platform, were the treasures in crockery, some half a dozen large wash-
bowls and a neat platter.

As we entered, the chief sat in state on a
small chest at one side of the fireplace, robed in
blue pants, a pink calico shirt, and, in graceful
folds, a navy blue blanket with a border of handsome crimson cloth edged with a row of large
pearl buttons. In his hair, which is crimped and
curls about his high forehead and hangs down his
back like a horsetail, was arranged the whole
skin of a white ermine. On the platform just
above him sat his wife with a similar blanket
about her and many silver bracelets on her arms.

Chilkat Tlingit House Interior

They showed us to our seats and expressed their pleasure in smiles and words. Our entire party occupied the honorable end of the room, but only we had the seats.

The old chief said he was so glad the minister had come at last! He wished it might have been when he was a boy; now he was old, he was soon to go down to death, but he could go more happily, knowing that his people would now have light.

He wished that the white man liked the Indian's food; then he would show us how they loved us. He had salmonberries: would we eat some? We consented, and a servant brought the wash bowls before the chief's wife, who with her hands filled up the bowls with the beautiful berries. The first was borne to us and set down on the floor before us, the next to Don-a-wok and Mrs. Dickinson, the others severally to groups of Indians in our party seated on the floor. We took

Stickeen Tlingit House Interior
(from A. Krause, *Die Tlingit Indianer*)

up our bowls and, after grace, began to eat with
our fingers. By this time a great many of the people had gathered. Mr. Willard spoke to them for
half an hour, after which, with singing and
prayer, we took our departure.

We then looked about the village, the houses
of which are ranged along the bluff about the
rapids. Running out from the walk in front of the
dwellings are trellises for drying salmon. Great
piles had already been put away, yet more were
drying. Below these, nearer the water, the people
were making fish oil in their wooden canoes. At
first, when I saw the boiling mass of fish, I won-
dered how they kept the canoe from burning.
Then I remembered that the fire was not under
the canoe but under a great altar-like mound of
stones, which, being made red hot, were dropped
into the canoe of fish. Out in the water were the
ingenious salmon traps, where the Indians take

immense quantities of the fish coming up the river at this season of the year to spawn.

Then, after a look at the beautiful lake of which the river is the outlet, Mr. Willard and I, with our interpreter, took the chief's canoe, and with two Indians to pole, we "shot" the rapids, seated one behind the other in the bottom of the boat, a hand on either side to steady us. I sat with my back to the head of the canoe and saw the dangers only to be thankful that we had escaped them, while Mrs. Dickinson, turned the other way and seeing always the rock we were to split upon, kept uttering cries of alarm. But it was only for a few minutes, and we reached the landing place.

We had dinner on a beach, then took the paddles for home, singing most of the way, our bodies full of weariness, but our hearts full of peace. Soon after nightfall we found ourselves at our own little home again.

But my letter is already too long, although I have not told you half that I wished. I must say "farewell" with the prayer that your small society may continue to grow in interest and influence...

CHILKAT MISSION
HAINES, ALASKA
AUGUST 24, 1881

What precious supplies the *U.S.S. Wachusette* has brought us!—books, papers, letters—comforting and helpful. We have so enjoyed them *all*...

I often realize the meaning of the Scripture "And a little child shall lead them," for truly our baby is a large element in the Chilkat mission force. For instance: The first day after our arrival here the children flocked in to see us. I had Baby on my lap, washing and combing her hair. The Indian children first shyly showed their black-and-red painted faces at a crack of the door after having taken a survey of the inside premises through a knothole. Baby smiled at them with me holding her wee thumb and first finger closely pinched together with a kiss. I had Kittie tell them that Baby was kissing them, and so baby won their first smile. They crept by slow degrees close up to us, watching the washing and combing process with open-mouthed interest.

After they had become thoroughly absorbed and I had put on Baby her pretty white apron, I had Kittie tell them that this was my baby, that she (Kittie) was my big girl, and that they all were my children. Just as I kept Baby, I wanted all my children kept—nice and clean. Had they ever seen a comb like that? No, they never had; so after grouping them in families, I gave each group a comb. You should have seen their faces! Such a study they were! Full of wonder and pleasure! For a moment they stood perfectly still, then with one accord ran out of the door and away.

In the course of fifteen minutes they began to reappear by twos and threes with faces ruddy and resplendent—the paint had been removed—and the hair, now combed, stood on end. Again were their faces a study as they arranged themselves before me with happy eyes. Of course I expressed delight and had them all sit down on the floor beside me while I taught them a hymn.

Thus the work began. From that day to this I have not seen the faces of those children painted, and day after day they regularly, of their own accord, present themseves to show me that they have combed their hair.

I have been so interested, too, in the effect of Baby's sweet face and winning ways on strangers who have come to us from the more distant villages. I have seen them enter with questioning, distrustful, suspicious faces, and in a few minutes melt into a restful enjoyment of the situation and go away with frank expression of their friendship and of pleasure at our coming. One old woman from the upper village had been waiting about the door outside, I know not how long, until I left the room for a moment. Then, slipping in, she sat down on the floor beside Baby and placed before her a basket of luscious berries. There the woman sat when I came out, not daring to raise her head, but smiling softly to herself. Going up, I knelt beside her and took her hand, telling her in Tlingit that I was glad to see her. She slowly looked up, and there was such a glad light in her face as she took my hand in hers and, patting softly, said something to me which Kittie interpreted as "my child, my child." Then she told me that she had never seen a white woman before and had felt afraid to come to see the minister's wife, but she wanted so much to come that she came with a present to the baby. Now she was afraid no more; she saw a friend's face.

And now you will be anxious to hear of peace prospects for Chilkat. I think favorable. As I told you in my last letter, the head chief, Shat-e-ritch, was ill and sent for and received of us medicines which seemed to do him good. On last Sabbath afternoon he came over the trail while we were holding services. Afterward he came into our home. He looked about suspiciously and seemed ill at ease. We showed him our house and its appointments. Then I had him sit at the table and take supper with us. The beans or something seemed to find the way to his heart; and then his heart came to his lips, and he told us that he had been told of bad things we said of him. We explained satisfactorily, and he went away apparently in the best humor and with the kindest feeling, asking me to take his daughter for my own and train her to be a good and wise woman. I declined to answer affirmatively as yet.

He gave us word that there was no actual fighting when he left Chilkat; that most of the people were anxious to have it settled so that they could come down here to school; that he had a long time prevented their fighting and they had promised to settle after the officer of the *Jamestown* came. But the day after Mr. Willard left, the "Murderer" (as he had long been called by the people) shot his own friend—one of the nobility, leaving only four—and that made the hearts of all the people sick, so that they had no strength and he wanted to say nothing to them. He had nothing to do with the fighting, only tried to prevent it and didn't like the man-of-war to come and talk so much with him about it. He wanted the officers to come and deal with those who fought and caused the fight. We explained to him that it was because he was for peace and was a wiser man than the fighters, that the officers wished to speak to him. He left for Chilkoot to buy oil for winter and returned yesterday, when we had another visit from him.

In the meantime, the *Wachusette* steamed along and cast anchor in our harbor. At first the Indians seemed frightened and suspicious. We rang a salute with our mission bell. The officers came ashore and to our house; then it grieved my heart to see the changed faces of the people. How their countenances were changed toward me! I looked in vain for the warm, welcoming smile as I passed among them. They were suspicious of us and averted their faces. But by degrees they were again inspired with confidence in the officers and us. We assured the people that the officers had come as friends to all who would do right. The captain invited them on board ship, and by and by flocks of canoes from the villages visited it and all became friends.

Captain Edward P. Lull had a conversation with Shat-e-ritch and sent for other counselors, who have not yet arrived. If they come in time for a talk tonight, the vessel will leave in the morning.

While Shat-e-ritch was in Chilkoot and before the steamer came, a party arrived from the upper Chilkat village with the word that peace was made, the satisfaction had been paid, and all were glad but one desperate man who would never be satisfied. We cannot tell as yet just how true this report may be.

On the other hand, that Sitka affair, of which I earlier wrote, is not considered as settled by the friends of the man who was injured and committed suicide in the prison. You remember I told you before that he had killed the man who had taken

Chief Don-a-wok
(from A. Krause, *Die Tlingit Indianer*)

his wife and then, because of the overwhelming disgrace, he took his own life. He was of the higher class of the lower village people, and the chief, Don-a-wok, is going to Sitka for satisfaction. He bought a large Hydah canoe for the trip. He also intends to bring back, as wife, the daughter of the chief. She is quite young, we hear, while Don-a-wok is a stalwart, dignified, and fine-looking man of perhaps fifty. His nephew, Cla-not, who will succeed him, is one of those who accompanied Dr. Jackson on his trip to Fort Simpson and to whom was first promised a missionary. He also was about the first to meet, recognize and welcome Dr. Jackson here.

These men are both interested in the Sitka affair, as the man was a relative of theirs. They

31

both are very friendly to us. We have had many talks, particularly with the older man, and last Sabbath Mr. Willard preached to him on "If ye forgive not men their trespasses, neither," etc. I had a long talk with him the other day. He has been very interested, as have all the people, in our house. I asked him if he were going to bring his new wife up here. "Yes," he said; he was going to sit down by the minister. Then I said, "I suppose you will build a new house like the white man's?" Yes, if he could get the lumber, he wanted to have an *upstairs*. He wanted Dr. Jackson to help him. I told him Mr. Willard would help him all he could in telling about the lumber and what he needed, and then I would show his wife how to arrange it nicely inside. I asked him if he were not going to marry his wife the Christian way and explained to him how that was and what it meant: one only and as long as life lasts; that he must take care of his wife as his own life, and she the same for him. No more two—always one. He seemed delighted and said he would bring her and be married the Christian way. I promised him that it should be in our pretty sitting room. His first wife has been dead a long time, and he seems to be honest and upright.

Cla-not is a splendid man physically and of good ability. He is the only man whom I know that has three wives; one who is much older than himself that he married for her wisdom. They are in the lower village. The only thing in the way of his coming at once to build here is that an uncle died leaving a house partly built, and it is a great point of honor among the Tlingit that the next male relative should take up the work—with all the giving of gifts and feasting which it entails—and finish the house, that it may stand as a monument to the memory of the deceased. So Cla-not has this to do. Then, he says, he will come here.

At present, besides our buildings and the trade-store shed, there are a few bark shelters and one open log hut—merely stopping places for the Indians when they come to trade—but these are crowded, and many more people will be here as soon as the winter's food is cured.

There is something delightful and comfortable in the coming of our American man-of-war on errands of peace! We like all the officers very much. The ship surgeon is from Carlisle, Pennsylvania; we at once claimed kinship with him.

Will you please send me those *Evangelists* and Sunday school papers, as you are through with them. We like to give the people one on Sunday. If you have anything which will help us in making Christmas remembered by the Indians, we would be glad to have them sent. Perhaps we would be able to get them if sent soon. We shall need some clothing, too—some shoes and stockings.

CHILKAT MISSION
HAINES, ALASKA
AUGUST 27, 1881

REV. SHELDON JACKSON, D.D., DEAR FRIEND AND BROTHER: I cannot refrain from dropping you a note of thanks, although words are too feeble to express our appreciation of what you have done in our behalf.

In the first place, you gained for us our hearts' desire—the appointment to preach glad tidings to the Chilkats. You advised and encouraged us by the way. We left home with the expectation of living in a tent until we could by our own labor put up a log house. This exposure your loving zeal and wise energy has prevented by taking upon your own shoulders a burden which, I trust, will soon be removed by interested people at home— the financial burden, I mean, for you have borne so much more than that in the planning and erection of the building which has given us such a comfortable home in this faraway land.

Your coming with us, too, and introducing us to the very chiefs to whom you first had promised a teacher years ago, has, I am sure, been most advantageous to the beginning of our work here, and your counsel and advice most helpful and comforting to us.

That God may bless you more and more abundantly in your labors of love is the prayer with thanksgiving of your grateful...

Carrie M. Willard

CHILKAT MISSION
HAINES, ALASKA
SEPTEMBER 12, 1881

REV. SHELDON JACKSON, D.D.: So much has occurred since we last wrote you that I despair of giving you a very full account. Don-a-wok, the chief, returned to his village last evening—so messengers tell us. But his heart is so sad that he could not come to us himself today; for, although his errand to Sitka was a prosperous one, the

Sitka Indians paying many blankets and Chinese trunks for the life of his friend, and while he had taken many more with him from home, yet he had not enough to satisfy the demand made as an honorable gift for his promised wife, and he was forced to come back without her. We are all sorry, for we had hoped much as a result of his example in marrying and making a home before his people. But it must be best somehow.

We made our anticipated tour of the villages, starting out on Thursday, first of September, and returning home on the following Tuesday. We at first intended to come back on Saturday and took with us only provision for that time. In addition, we carried our blankets, etc. We found that at high tide a canoe could be brought quite inland, within a mile of our house, by a winding stream, which after a labyrinthine course at length found its way to the river Chilkat. So I felt brave in my short flannel dress to undertake the tramp.

Billy Dickinson had taken his canoe across the trail early in the morning, and at noon, after an early lunch, we took up the march. Baby went on before with Billy, Sam and Mr. Willard, each with his pack; Kittie with a little bundle, Mrs. Dickinson's two little Indians with her luggage, and she and I bringing only our own selves. It was a beautiful day, cool and bright. The scenery was of almost bewildering beauty.

I longed to stop only to enjoy it the more, yet new features constantly urged us forward. The scene was as if in the tropics, great-leaved plants and ferns, both delicate and monstrous, fruit, flowers, and vines on every side, alders dipping their boughs into still, shady waters, while the dark pines, all festooned with moss, overshadowed the whole. Again the trail led into beautiful pasture-land with clumps of trees so like the home fruit trees that it made my heart jump. We crossed Mr. Willard's hay field where the sweet-smelling hay stood in shocks awaiting the completion of the goat house we are building of logs.

At last we struck the stream, at first just wide enough for the canoe, which was a frail, shaky thing. Billy took the prow and paddle; Mrs. Dickinson the stern, to steer. I sat in the bottom of the middle of the canoe and had work enough before we reached the village. There was a strong wind and the water was rough, as here the river becomes wide—a mile and a half. The big waves shipped us plenty of sea, and, as we sometimes struck them, our crazy little boat yawed quite perceptibly. It kept me busy dipping to keep her afloat. I was thankful that Baby was safe with her father, as the others had all kept the trail.

After a tedious voyage we reached the lower village about five p.m., wet and chilled. The others had arrived before us, and, although Don-a-wok was away, his servant girl had opened and swept his house for us. Freshly washed gravel lay on the hearth, and she was lighting a fire. I soon exchanged my wet clothes for dry ones, then set about getting supper. Presents of fish and berries began to come in, and we had an abundant meal. Then came a good little feather bed for me, and all the people began to flock in, eager to see and hear. We had about sixty-five Indians present and gave them a service.

We slept on the floor about the great central fire, with the stars shining down on us through the many openings in the roof, for it is a rickety old house and small—not at all like the chief's in Chilkoot. A perfect gale blew before morning, and it seemed as though the timbers, which are tied together by thongs and bark, would certainly blow in upon us, but I judge they have stood many a stronger storm. We hired two canoes next day to take us to the upper villages.

This canoeing is an experience. The canoe is hewn from one tree, so narrow for its length. It is admirably adapted to these waters, but unsteady. We all sit single file in the bottom of the boat.

The first part of the way we went bravely with full sails, afterward very laboriously, the Indians poling at times, and again wading and dragging the canoe. The water is very shallow in places and the current fearful.

We reached the first village at seven o'clock, hungry, cold and tired, not knowing what quarters we might find for the night. The people were busy with salmon, and the houses very crowded with fish and strangers who had come to fish, but there was a large house in the course of erection, with planks fastened on the sides, the roof consisting of rafters; the turf fresh and green for the floor. Windows we had no need of, and there was a door. It was cordially opened, and we soon had a fire blazing.

The owner of the house was so pleased to have us occupy his new house that he sent wash bowls full of berries and fish oil, also fresh salmon, and we partook of a bountiful supper.

But cooking by such a fire is slow, particularly when subject to many interruptions, as the traveling missionary has. So, after our meal and the many greetings and little speeches, we were too weary to do more than sing the people a hymn and bid them come to an early morning meeting. Our Indians reared their sails on their poles against the side of the building to form a shed for our blankets, and there we found refreshing sleep.

Next morning, after early breakfast of salmon roasted on a stick, bread, butter and coffee, we had a sunrise meeting of about seventy-five Indians who gave almost breathless attention. Then, bidding them good-bye and receiving their hearty thanks, we urged them again to come to our place and build where they could have school and regular service. Then we once more took our canoe, with borrowed poles of stronger make than our own—for the rapids lay before us—and were soon on our way to Klukwan, the uppermost village. We did not know what awaited us, for we had learned on the way that the trouble, which had been smoothed over in the presence of the man-of-war, had broken out again, and that the people were in the midst of war.

We felt the greater necessity of hastening forward, trusting that we would be given the ears and hearts of the people. We did not trust in vain. Oh, how thankful we have been that we did thus go on! We found the people troubled; we brought them comfort. We found them warring, and we brought them peace.

We found Klukwan by far the largest Indian village we have seen in Alaska, and the richest and most substantially built, many of the houses elegant in their way. The carvings in many are worth thousands of blankets. Three of the largest of these houses belong to Shat-e-ritch, and the largest and costliest one he has given to the mission. In it we held our Sunday service. The next in value, the chief's treasure-house, was made our lodging place. We found many of the houses turned into forts with barricades in plenty.

There are four distinct tribal families—the Wolves and Whales, who are nearly connected; and the Crows and Cinnamon Bears, who are connected in like manner by intermarriages. It is not lawful for those of the same family to intermarry, though a man may have a woman and her daughter both to wife.

The war has been between the Whales and the Crows, of differing castes and thus creating much aggravated touble. Of all the people, the Whales have most of our sympathy. They are smaller in numbers and comparatively poorer. They are afraid to move out of their houses and are literally prisoners in their homes. Signs of mourning are on every hand: the beautiful hair of the women cut close to the head and their faces blackened; the carvings covered with red matting; the box and moccasins of their dead placed on a shelf over the door from which they went out never to return.

We held a separate meeting for the Whales in the afternoon in the house where the whole trouble began, as they could not come to the other.

First, the eldest son murdered a Crow and then ran away to the Stick country. The Crows retaliated. Then the second son made some show of revenge, so that they demanded his life. His wife, who was Crow, defended and protected him. The poor old mother's heart was broken with sorrow. She called on her son to give himself up, but in vain. She even followed the first son to the interior on the same quest. Not succeeding, she returned, and, dressing themselves in their best, she and her daughter went out and demanded to be shot, that the honor of their family might be maintained. They perished at the hands of the Crows. At last the son came to the door and gave himself up, with his wife clinging to him. She begged that he be allowed to descend to the foot of the steps, that his body might not fall and be bruised. The Crows suspected her of treachery, as she had so long shielded him, so they shot her, although she was a Crow. I believe her husband was afterward killed.

When we entered the house, the only remaining member of the household sat on the floor, his head on his knees and an old hat drawn over it—a young man, but one who had evidently lost the hope and power of youth. Into that house we brought the gospel of light and peace.

A way was opened for us to a man in one of the forts upon whose death or recovery hangs the settlement of the matter between the tribes. We found him very sick and ministered to him as best we could, as to both temporal and spiritual things.

A Crow family had lost a son by death after an illness, and they had just returned from the cremating of the body when we arrived. We brought them word of that world to them so full of mystery. Mr. Willard preached for an hour and a half, showing them how they were living in antagonism to God.

Shat-e-ritch is of higher caste than any other chief of the Chilkats, being a Cinnamon Bear and very rich. He occupies a neutral position in this trouble, except as he is connected with the Crows and tries to make peace, though his power does not extend over any but his own tribe.

He received us first into his own house, giving us the place of honor. He soon inquired as to how long we expected to stay. Informing him that we intended to go back that afternoon (for the current is so swift that we could come down in two or three hours, but it requires one and sometimes two days to go up), we were told that the people's hearts would be sick if we did not stay over Sunday with them. We then told him that we had no food for that time or we would gladly stay. He replied that Mrs. Dickinson, our interpreter, could speak for Indian or white man. She must command his house—ask for whatever we needed. His wife brought out wheat flour and baking powder and made bread. They sent us everything that we could require and gave us new blankets and pillows for bedding, fixing us up in the treasure-house. Several others brought and sent in berries and salmon at different times. Tradition demands a full equivalent for every gift they make; still they give freely, and it is pleasant to receive.

On Sabbath, Shat-e-ritch called the head men to his house to a feast for the purpose of making Baby and me Cinnamon Bears and settling on the names they should give us. Toward evening they brought me my name and the presents began to pour in from all my relatives, gray-haired men and women calling me "aunt" and calling Baby "aunt." They had given me the highest name ever held by Cinnamon Bears: *Nauk-y-stih*; and Baby's is next in honor: *Tling-get Sawye K-Cotz-e.*

Generations ago the Cinnamon Bear people first saw copper coming in bits on the wrecks of vessels. It was the greatest of wonders to the people, and they prized it more than gold. No man could get enough skins or blankets to pay for more than the least little pieces of it. Thousands of blankets were required to pay for them, and the Cinnamon Bears' greatest ambition was to get these bits together in a carving of the Cinnamon Bear's head, which would bind them strongly together and make one whole of the many mites. This is the meaning of my name, the Cinnamon Bear's head holding together and making one treasure of these bits of copper.

I wish you could have seen them as they told me of this, gathered in that great dark house with its hundreds of carved vessels and boxes of blankets and oil and every other Indian treasure, their strong, earnest, kindly features lighted up from within by love, and from without by the crackling, blazing fire in the middle of the room. They sat about, and I stood before them touched by this demonstration. When they were through, I answered that my heart was full; surely they were my brothers.

They had told me the meaning of my name, and now I, the first white woman that had ever borne it, wished to tell them the new and even more precious meaning which I wished it to bear henceforth. All the Chilkat people were to me the most priceless bits of copper. Their bitterness had kept them apart; the bits were owned by enemies. Now love was brought, enough to buy them all. They had made *me* the great Cinnamon Bear's head to bind all these precious pieces into one. Now there should be no more pieces, no more enemies, but all one, till at last the Nauk-y-stih, with all the bits of copper which made it such a treasure, should be borne to the great Chief above.

The meaning of Baby's name is *a mighty city* where all the people are exempt from sickness, sorrow and poverty—all are great.

We came away on Monday loaded with presents and the thanks of the people. We stopped a few moments, without leaving our canoes, at the middle village. Here my new relatives had heard of my name and came out bearing me still other presents of dried berry cake and dried salmon.

It soon began to rain and blow. The waves tossed our canoe and the spray dashed over us, wetting the entire crew. Many times it seemed almost impossible to reach the shore that day, but we did, and in safety.

It was too stormy to attempt crossing the bar that day; so we took up our quarters in Don-a-wok's house again, where we were sheltered from the wind, even though rain came through. We had another delightful meeting there, and next day reached home, where we found all safely kept.

We were tired, but none of us sick. All kept safe and well through storm and sea and war, and God gave us great peace. We did not take the least cold—not even Baby, who enjoyed the trip in her way as much as any of us. And I assure you we did enjoy it all. Even danger was robbed of its terror...

Don-a-wok was here today. He seemed sad, but we see reason for rejoicing even in what is a trial to him, for he is standing by his principles. It seems that the bride which was to have been was willing to come with him, and all her friends were satisfied with the exception of one sister, who demanded a slave from Don-a-wok. He had onceowned slaves, but some time ago he and Shat-e-ritch made their slaves free; so Don-a-wok refused to give a slave and lost his wife.

The trip to Sitka seems to have done the Indians good. They saw the bright school there, old and young learning to read. Mr. Willard assured them that if they would only now come together and set to work they could have a school superior to that of Sitka. They seem anxious to do so.

Don-a-wok is a chief of the Crows, but of the two lower villages. They have nothing to do with the fighting in the uppermost village. Neither do the Crows of Chilkoot, who are also friendly to us and peaceable. Don-a-wok claims Mr. Willard as his brother and is going to name him soon.

While we were away we discovered some needs; one was a large handbell for calling the people together. In lieu of it, Mr. Willard and I made a tour of the village, house by house, when we were ready to have them come to meeting.

Another need for our school is maps of the United States and world, a globe, and an organ for our church and school. The people like music and learn quickly the tunes we have taught them word by word and note by note, but you would hardly recognize our old familiar hymns. The singers' voices are so strong and they sing with such a will that my voice makes no impression at all. I cannot stem such a flood, but an instrument would help. Our piano is for our house and cannot be moved back and forth. We must also have a mission canoe. We have the largest mission field in Alaska and in many respects the most important. We must go by canoe to reach most of our people, and it costs five to ten dollars every trip. Mr. Willard expects to go this winter by skates and snowshoes, but when the river becomes navigable in the spring we expect to make rounds monthly. We already see good of our first trip and feel this itinerant work is important. It must be done before we get the people in any numbers to come. In time we trust that this will become the center, but it will be a long time, for the people have good houses and are loath to leave them. Some, indeed, are *now* ready to come, but they are a small minority, and there is much difficulty as yet about getting ready lumber. It requires an enormous amount of labor to build as they do.

SEPTEMBER 26

Still no steamer. We have been in daily expectation of her arrival for three weeks, but oh so thankful that our Sabbaths were not broken by her coming! We are having beautiful weather.

We have good news from the upper village! After we left they began to make peace. The last affray was promptly paid for in blankets. The wounded man, upon whose fate so much hung in getting a settlement, is now rapidly recovering.

The Crows took into their houses the young man in whose house we held service for the Whales, treating him to the best of everything they possessed, having him eat and sleep with them. The Whales took into their homes, in the same way, the great Crow terror, "the murderer." This is their way of expressing satisfaction, confidence and peace, and now feasting and dancing are going on. The lower villages have joined them in this. Many of the villagers have promised to come down to us here when the feasting is over.

We hope to begin regular indoor work by October first. We are anxious to learn the language, for there is much we long to say which we cannot get others to say for us. Mr. Dickinson is a kind friend. His wife has told him to go on and leave her here until we learn to speak a little, but he will not do that. Kittie is to go back to the Home by the first opportunity. So if the Dickinson's do go, we will be the only whites and only persons in Chilkat country who speak English.

CHILKAT MISSION
HAINES, ALASKA
OCTOBER 24, 1881

TO THE PRESBYTERIAN SABBATH SCHOOL IN EAST SPRINGFIELD, NEW YORK, MY DEAR FRIENDS: Three eventful months have passed since our former letter, written from Sitka, when we knew but little more of our present home and work than did you. Now we are domiciled and almost as much at home as though we had been born here.

Carrie M. Willard Among the Tlingits

In Fort Wrangell and Sitka the missionaries are housed in buildings erected and occupied by the Russian government during its rule, but in the Chilkat country, no white men had ever lived except the trader who preceded us a few months, the husband of our interpreter, Mrs. Dickinson. When we left home, it was with a knowledge of this fact and with the expectation of living in tents until we could get out logs and put up such a house as we could. Dr. Sheldon Jackson made this unnecessary by giving us the needed help.

Two weeks after our arrival here—July 18th— our friends Drs. Jackson and Corlies, with the three carpenters, left us. Our house was incomplete, but the frame was up and the roof on, the floor laid and some of the doors hung. So we came right into it and went on with the work: carpentering, cabinet making (for we brought no furniture with us save one chair, a little stand and the stove), garden grubbing, tree felling, and stable building from logs, quarters for our goats (a pair of which we brought with us from Sitka to supply our baby with milk), cutting grass for the goats' winter food with case and pocket knives (for a scythe was overlooked in our outfit), receiving the Indians who came in to see the things the minister had brought, cutting garments for them and trying to help their sick, preaching, etc., almost without end, as it seems to us still. So busy are we, and so much work yet to do. With all this, we have made a tour of our villages—four in number; and this brings me back to the main subject.

Before leaving Sitka we intended to locate in the upper village, thirty miles up the Chilkat

River, as it is the largest of the four. But finding that we could not get the lumber up—the river was low—we decided on this as the best point the district afforded, although four and a half miles from the nearest village. Except for a few bark huts the Indians put up last winter, the only building besides our own is the trading post. If we could have spoken the language, we would have gone to the upper village and opened a school—for this winter, at least; but we have a year's hard work before us in getting fixed up and studying the language. It seems the best plan to build a mission village here. In the first place, we secure those of the people who are most in earnest to hear and learn. In this way, too, we keep our work largely free from the jealousies of tribe and village chiefs. This is the "minister's place," as the people call it, and all are free to come without compromising tribal relations.

The nearest of the three villages on Chilkat River is coming over in a body to see us. The people there have been very busy getting ready to come. Their annual food supply food is mostly gathered in September and consists principally of dried salmonberries and salmon oil. They have potatoes, too, which had to be dug and housed. Now all is complete, we hear, and they will soon be with us. The bulk of their provisions will be left until heavy snowfall, when the people travel with greater ease on snowshoes. Some from each of the other villages have promised to come soon.

It is too late in the season now for them to do much in the way of building. We must be content to have homes as growth allows. Perhaps some day there will be a mission steamer in Alaskan waters which will convey lumber from the mission mill to mission villages for prices which will enable the Indians to build comfortable houses.

We have word today that Don-a-wok has taken a wife, or rather a child who is to be his wife in the course of time. When a couple are married, they adopt a boy and a girl to train up in their own ways, to take their place in the event of death. If the husband dies first, the boy becomes the husband to the widow. If the wife is taken first, the girl takes her place. Thus we often see a young boy with a decrepit wife, and old men in their dotage sometimes have mere child-wives. In case there is no such successor provided for, the friends of the deceased partner claim the right to appoint one from their own number. This was the whole trouble, as we believe, in Don-a-wok's case. His failure to secure the wife he wanted from a stranger-tribe resulted, no doubt, from intrigue on the part of his connections here, who were determined to make him take his former wife's nieces. They wished him to take *two* of them, but he refused, saying that the minister did not like such marriages. He said he would not do it, but he yielded so far as to take one—a girl about thirteen years old. She is called his wife, and he has taken her into his house to care for her, but they will probably not be married for two or three years. He is eager to have her go to school.

None of the maps of Alaska that we have seen give any idea of the Chilkat country. Lynn Canal is shown, and we are located at its head, where, indenting the western shore, is our Portage Bay.

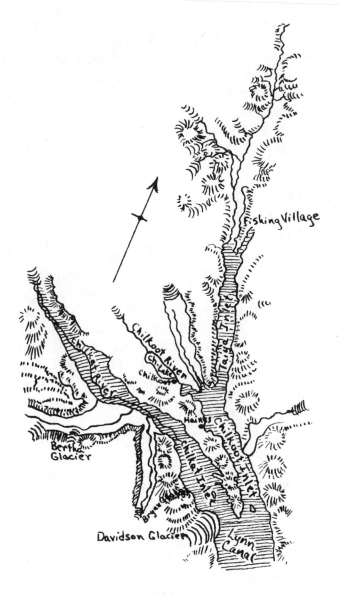

Chilkat Mission Region
(facsimile of Carrie M. Willard map)

Just to the north is the mouth of Chilkoot River, which rises in a beautiful lake of the same name about ten miles distant and near which stands the Chilkoot village. Chilkat River is something over a mile to the westward and is a mile and a half wide. It joins the canal about seven miles south, so that, while by trail or portage it is but little more than four miles to the lower Chilkat village, it is more than fifteen miles by water. The little peninsula formed by this large river and the canal is the largest level tract which we have seen in Alaska and is quite good soil. We hope in time to make it a mission farm and to induce the Indians to raise food. There is good ground enough to produce bread and beef for the entire present population of the thirty-mile strip.

While our immediate surroundings are almost flat, the country generally is mountainous and picturesque in the extreme. When we came in July, the whole of Chilkat Peninsula was one mass of flowers and vines. In places the vegetation was almost tropical for richness. One's steps sank into the wealth of mosses and this though the sun rose and set in ice, for the mountains which guard us on every hand are crowned with everlasting snow—some fifteen glaciers being visible from our windows.

Our first snowstorm this fall came on the twenty-first of September. On the twenty-sixth of that month, ice formed in our barrel of rainwater one-fourth of an inch in thickness. So, you see, our climate here differs very much from that of Sitka or Wrangell. We are almost beyond influence of the Japanese current.

Our school was opened on August 8th, but owing to the distance from the villages and the fall work of the people, the attendance has been small so far—often not more than two or three; but these have been taught. One fellow, whom we call Willis, is particularly bright and faithful. He brings dried salmon to do him through the week and sleeps in Mr. Dickinson's woodhouse.

Getting in the salmon is quite a festival with the Indians. At the close of the season, they have much feasting and dancing. When Willis went over to the village for his week's provision, the people tried to persuade him to stay and enjoy the fun with his brothers, sisters, and friends; but his answer was "I am going back to the minister's place," and the little fellow has resolutely adhered to his purpose. He is only ten or eleven years old, can read easy English lessons, and recites all the tract primer catechism. One other boy—Mark, son of one of the succeeding chiefs—has learned the letters also. We have promised each a book when we can get books. We hope to have a pleasant Christmas, though we have no presents.

Mr. Willard has preached twice each Sabbath, besides our preaching tours to the villages and the occasions when we caught a company through the week, and always to attentive, often eager, listeners.

We are seeing already a few triumphs over witchcraft and the power of the medicine men and have had some precious bits of encouragement. First a man came in with much eagerness and earnestness, saying that he had started off in his canoe to hunt mountain sheep, but when he had gone some distance, the little boat turned over and he lost his gun. He wanted us to pray that he might recover it. Mr. Willard explained to him the nature of prayer and miracle and that he must not expect God to cause the water to throw up the weapon, but that he would ask God to give the man strength and wisdom to find the gun. The man said he did not expect a miracle, but he wanted God's help so when the tide was out and the water low he might see the gun and get it up.

Soon after, a young man came to ask the minister to pray that God would turn the heart of the woman he loved so that she would marry him, for he loved her so that if she did not marry him, he did not know what he would do with himself. We told him that we would ask God to do so if it would be best, but we could not tell if it would be.

Afterward a man from Chilkoot came to us in great distress; his son was dying, and he wanted us to ask God to spare the boy's life and make him well. He wanted us also to give him some food and clothing to put out for the use of the spirit should the boy die. The Chilkats believe in another life and another world, but that between this world and the other lies a great distance, much land and then a great green water of which no one can drink. When a good spirit at last reaches the shore of this water, the inhabitants of the good world come with canoe and bear him over, while the very wicked are doomed never to cross. When a person dies, if the body is burned, the spirit passes with comfortable warmth through the intervening space. That the spirit may have every comfort on the long journey, the people put out or burn with the body both food and clothing. A person who dies by drowning is forever cold and unhappy.

After explaining to the father the true way, we knelt down with him and the Indians he had with him and prayed. Some days after, he came again. I never saw a greater change in anyone's appearance in so short a time. He bounded into the house, his face full of joy. He said, "It is true about your God. My child is better." Then he told us of how, when he went from here that day, the people were all crying and mourning for the child's death. The Indian doctors had said that the boy would not get well—could not live. They all thought him dead already, he had so long lain in that stupor. But the father—oh, how he prayed to God to spare that child! At last a woman came in and said the child was not dead, and by and by the boy came to himself, looked about and spoke. And now he was getting well, and just as soon as he was well enough, they were coming to the minister's place to live, so that they could go to school and learn more. He said that they believed no more in the Indian doctor. They had paid him ten blankets (thirty dollars) for nothing—a sore reflection, I assure you, especially to a Chilkat, for they are very shrewd at a bargain.

Let me give you an instance. This afternoon a man came with three ducks, with an innocent air, saying he brought them for a present, and then as is their custom, sat to wait for his *pay-present*. Mr. Willard gave him the exact price, and the man smiled and departed. When I came to unfeather the birds, I found but one fit to use. The fellow knew we could not refuse a present and he would be sure of his pay, whereas if he had brought them to sell, we would have discovered the quality of the goods and bade him begone. It is a custom we have seemed obliged to observe.

We need your prayers, dear friends, for wisdom, love, patience, and strength...

Carrie M. Willard

CHILKAT MISSION MANSE
HAINES, ALASKA
OCTOBER 28, 1881

MY DEAR FRIENDS: We have given up the steamer till next spring, but we know that He who careth for the sparrows knows and cares for all our needs.

OCTOBER 30

What do you think I have to write tonight? Just when I didn't know what to put in my baby's mouth we looked out and beheld the steamer *Favorite* entering our bay at about eleven o'clock.

The steamer did not bring our piano—too heavy, the officers said—so it is in Sitka. But oh! oh! oh! the splendid mail they brought and did give us today—"three bags full; one for the master, one for the dame, etc." We have been reading and reading till we are so full of every feeling that it is very difficult to get any of it into action.

The yeast came, for which I am thankful. I did not bring any with me, for that which I had planned to bring was not dry enough and was to be sent by mail afterward. We have gotten along, but now we will have some good bread, and I

Chilkats Making Fish Oil
(from A. Krause, *Die Tlingit Indianer*)

think there will be butter in the freight. The gingham came and such a treasure in books! Exactly
the kind we had wished for but did not hope to
get. Oh, so many thanks to all! If our friends at
home only knew how welcome are their letters
and their tokens of loving thoughtfulness when
received here in our loneliness, they would feel
rewarded for sending them to us...

The Indians make fish oil in their canoes. The
canoes are half buried in the earth and filled with
fish and water. Alongside, stones are built up like
an altar, under which a roaring fire is kept until
the stones become red hot. Then they are dropped
into the canoe. The fish are boiled in this way to a
jelly, then allowed to stand. Much of the oil rises
and is skimmed off. The rest is rolled in matting,
placed on a frame over the canoe and pressed by
the bare feet of the women.

This oil is a highly esteemed article of food
among the Indians. They dip their dried salmon

into it and also preserve a certain red berry in it. An Indian is happy with a large horn spoon and a washbowl of berries in oil before him. How they slip down without choking him is wonderful. His spoon holds a dipperful, and with a peculiar grace he raises it to his lips and in an instant the contents disappear, scarcely disturbing a muscle.

NOVEMBER 1

We had about seventy Indians at service yesterday. Thursday Mr. Willard had taken one of the medicine men and a chief to his study, where we keep the sewing machine, and explained its workings to them. We have been coming into closer and closer contact with the medicine men and chiefs and gradually but surely approaching conflict. We knew it would come sooner or later— just as soon as they felt our power gaining ascendency over theirs with the people. Just what sort of a conflict it might be we could not forecast.

I have spoken before of the sick being brought to us. There has been much sickness among the people this fall. Some have died, but, thanks be to God! not one of the many we have tended.

During the past week our hands and hearts have been more than full with people coming in from all the villages with their sick and dying in canoes, saying that they had heard of the true God and no longer believed in the Indian doctors. Others say they have given the medicine men everything they had and were so poor that no blanket remained to cover the dying child.

Friday, one poor woman brought to us her baby of three years. It had been sick for a year

Tlingit Rattle
(from A. Krause, *Die Tlingit Indianer*)

and was a living skeleton. I never felt so sick at
heart over any human being as over that little
burning-eyed creature who, moaning at every
breath and literally dying, was carried to us. The
mother told us the sad story—how the family had
given everything, dishes, blankets and all; how
the medicine men had sung, rattled, charmed, ate
fire, etc., but all to no purpose. With tears she
said, "Oh, help me, help me! My children are all I
have." I worked with the little one all afternoon,
and he seemed better and is still so.

There were many others, but I must tell you
of only one. Yesterday morning, Sabbath, among
the group of patients waiting in the kitchen was a
woman who begged me to come and see her boy
who was dying. After disposing of the others and
getting the house righted, I left Baby with papa
and followed the woman, taking with me what I
had in the house that might be necessary. But I
had nothing for proper food for the child. We had
tried to buy oatmeal at the store when ours
failed, but they would not sell it. I found the child
in what seemed to me to be a dying condition—

unable to move, with cold limbs and hot head, the only action apparent in the little body being the spasmodic jumping of the throat and upper part of the chest and the rolling of the eyes. I had them give me blankets and put on water to heat; then got brandy and went to work. I found that the child had taken no food for ten days, and immediately I dispatched a messenger to the store saying that they must sell or give me some oatmeal and condensed milk. I would take no refusal; they must give it. I soon had the pleasure of feeding the famished child milk and in awhile some gruel. Seeing him in a better condition, I left him and went to church with my sunbonnet and apron on and led the singing.

After putting Baby to sleep, and with dinner over, I lay down for half an hour and then went back, finding the boy no better, if not worse, than he was in the morning. The medicine doctors had been in talking to them, saying all manner of things—that all their dreams said the child would die, etc.; that if he got well they would cut off their hair and do nothing more; that they would believe in God if He showed Himself so strong as to heal that boy. You may be sure with this double motive I worked and prayed, and at bedtime, when I left him again, he was much better. After taking the medicine I had left him, he rested, slept through much of the night, and this morning is perhaps a little better but still very sick indeed. I do not know how it is going. I can only do my best. I believe that however it goes, it will somehow be for His praise, and in that I shall be more than satisfied.

Yesterday a medicine doctor's wife followed me into the house of this sick child and sat near the door constantly making sneering remarks. This morning her husband came out as I passed his house and commenced talking at a tremendous rate, gesticulating and speaking angrily till he got so close to me as to shake his fist within two inches of my face. I am not afraid of him nor of all of them. As long as there are sick whom I can benefit, I shall do my duty without a thought of the old doctors, except to hope and pray that they may be convinced and converted. May that day come soon! One of the doctors is here now to get me to do something for him. I have been having a talk with him.

Our freight has been gotten into the house from the boat this morning. But now, with much love to all, I must close. The boat leaves us soon.

Carrie M. Willard

CHILKAT MISSION MANSE
HAINES, ALASKA
NOVEMBER 30, 1881

MY DEAR FRIENDS: You can scarcely realize how those few words of yours in regard to the increase of zeal for missions among the people at home strengthened and helped us. We have much to encourage us and cause for rejoicing with thanksgiving; yet there are times when it is hard to keep only these things before us. Thus, such sympathy as yours is very sweet.

There has been a great deal of sickness among our people—a terrible eruptive disease much like smallpox, though not fatal. A number of deaths occurred, however, before the people began to come to us to build their homes. Since they came, bringing their sick with them in canoes, four deaths have taken place, but we have the infinite joy of believing that all are saved and happy souls today. They were two babes, a young woman, and a dear boy—the one I wrote of in my last letter. I was with the sick ones almost day and night for awhile, particularly with this boy who died and with a woman who has recovered. After it became impossible for me to go to the village, the children who could be carried were brought to the house. For one of the babies who had died first I had done much, and I hoped the babe would get well. But oh, it is such unequal warfare, this battling with death in the people's houses with wind, snow, or smoke constantly present.

I cannot tell you what I felt when these babies died. That their lives should be spared seemed almost essential to the success of our work here. You know how the case stood after Mr. Willard's preaching against their witchcraft and superstitions and then bringing party after party—medicine men, chiefs and others—into our house. We showed them the machinery of sewing machine and clock and told them of the more intricate machinery of the human body. We were trying to show the people the absurdity of believing that if the body got out of order in their hands someone had bewitched it. If some dirt got into the fine wheels of a watch, did they think that the medicine men could charm it into running order without removing that obstruction? How much less power could they have over the human body!

After this, I say, many of them brought their sick to us. Of course the doctors were enraged at the loss of their gains and predicted that our patients would die. We worked with an almost agonizing zeal and felt the sick must not die. After many days and sad nights of anxious working, watching and praying, when it seemed as if a feather's weight might turn the balance, it was turned: the boy began to recover rapidly for some time, regaining appetite and strength.

Then I was not able to go any more, and the next thing I heard was that he was worse, then dead. I felt stunned; I could not believe it. I had felt so sure that he would get well. I could not say a word. It seemed as though everything that had been accomplished would now be lost, and yet I could not a moment doubt God's sovereignty, wisdom, or love. I must just be still.

We had heard before that if the boy died, his parents would hide the death from us, for they meant to cremate the body. We expected that the medicine men would do their best to inflame the people against us. But instead, the parents came in the burden of their grief, telling us of the glad departure of the little spirit and that they were not nearly so sick at heart because they were sure that he had gone to be with Jesus. Not one word of reproach, even where we had expected charges and demands for "satisfaction!" They told us of the boy's talk, prayers, and singing of the hymns he loved, dying with the lines on his lips.

Day after day he had pleaded to be carried to the schoolhouse, but he was not fit to be moved. On Sabbath when the bell rang, he would beg them to take him to the church. We often had little meetings in the house for him.

The parents said they wanted to have him buried like a Christian. So on Sabbath his body was borne to the schoolhouse he had so longed to enter. Mr. Willard preached on the resurrection. The people seemed profoundly impressed.

It is the Tlingits' custom after the death of a friend to eat nothing for days, to paint their faces black, to cut their hair close, and to wear shabby clothing. But this mother came to the funeral with clean face and dress.

Many of the people say that they do not wish to burn any more of their dead. We did not insist on burial and indeed have said little about it, but we do prefer they bury their dead because they cannot do so without disregarding their superstitions, for their belief is that the spirit whose body is not burned suffers an eternity of cold.

This was not our first funeral. The first was when the baby died. Broken-hearted, the mother came to me. She had four children, and this was the first death. Her heart seemed to have been won through what we had tried to do for the little one, and she wanted to know what she ought to do. The old people talked terribly about burying. The grandmother gave the mother no peace at all, saying the child should be cremated, but the mother wanted to do as we said. I sat down and talked with her, explaining to her what the Bible tells us of life and death. She then said that she wanted to have the body buried, but her friends did not and she could not tell them all. She wished the minister would talk to them. So they were called together, and Mr. Willard gave them a long plain talk. They said at last that for their "mother Nauk-y-stih's sake" they would bury the child if we would show them how.

Mr. Willard made a small coffin, and we covered it with white. I made a shroud for the child and had them bring the body to me to dress and put in the box. The body was already prepared as they prepare the corpse, the face all covered with vermilion, mittens on the hands, the knees drawn up and tied against the body. In the people's sight I washed the paint from its face, smoothed the hair and put on a dress. It was snowing when they laid the little one away, and it seemed as though the parents' hearts would break. It was the first breach of their oldtime customs made dear to them through generations.

The grandmother had not given up. She made them suffer at home with her revilings. Several times it seemed as though they must yet take up the body and burn it. They came to us for comfort and strength. We feel more hopeful of their salvation than of that of any other family of our people.

Mr. Willard hopes to form a class for instruction of those who really desire to be Christians. We ask the prayers of our dear friends at home…

Carrie M. Willard

CHILKAT MISSION MANSE
HAINES, ALASKA
DECEMBER 13, 1881

MY DEAR FRIENDS: I did not tell you in my last letter what had been done by the man-of-war.

This time the *Wachusette* was commanded by Captain Henry Glass. He called for the head men to come to him. Only two of the higher chiefs he invited into the cabin. He gave them a forcible exposition of the law:

1. That he would punish anyone who made, sold or introduced any intoxicating drink or anything of which to make it.
2. That if they had any fighting and anyone was killed, he would be here immediately. The murderer would be seized, taken below in irons and tried. If proved guilty, he would be hanged as any white man would be.
3. If they harmed the whites who came among them, he would storm the Indian village and blockade their river.

He showed them what the big guns were made of by firing a number of balls and bombshells, which shook our house although sent in an opposite direction.

Another child has been called away—one who had been sick for a year or more—and this morning the body was burned. This was the second cremation since our coming.

While we were at breakfast, Esther, the mother of the boy of whom I wrote you as having been buried from the church, came in looking sad and saying that her heart was sick. Ever since her boy had been put in the ground the Indians had troubled her so that she could neither eat nor sleep. They were taunting her in every way.

They had tried to induce her to have the body disinterred and cremated. This morning before they started to the other child's burning, the people crowded into her house and besieged her with new force. At last Esther's mother (and this is remarkable because as a rule the old people are tied to their traditional customs) said to them, "No, we will not do it. As for me, I have only just begun to learn about God, but I want to go to him and to my grandchild when I die. And I want to tell you all now that when I die I don't want you to burn my body. I want to be buried."

Then Esther made a similar declaration. Then Chief Don-a-wok—Esther's uncle—told them that he wanted them all to remember, too, that his body was not to be burned when he died. He wanted the minister to bury him.

After this the people left the house, but Esther's heart was so sick that she felt as if she would die. Her mother told her to put on her blanket and go up to the minister's. So she came, though she hadn't wanted to come for a long time because the people talked so. She fears that she is not going to live long, and she wanted to ask us to be sure to bury her and to take care of her little boy, the only child left her.

I had a long comforting talk with her and kept her here all day, engaging her on sewing which I'd given her for herself. Tonight she went home quite cheerful. It seemed to encourage her when I told her what martyrs had suffered and what was promised to those who endure persecution.

Mr. Willard witnessed the doctors' dance some time ago. It is a sort of exorcism. Almost all sickness among the Indians is regarded as the result of witchcraft. The medicine man is called, and for ten blankets, he will scatter the evil spirits. If the spirits are obstinate and the person dies, he accuses someone of having bewitched the dead person. For certain other blankets, the medicine man will tell by divination who the witch is. We were told that the latter is then taken, and, with his feet tied together and his hands tied behind his back, is shut up with the corpse and burned with it or left to starve, unless there are relatives rich enough to pay for the exorcism of the evil spirit. Since we have been here this has never gone so far as a pointing out of the witch.

You have read a description in Dr. Jackson's *Alaska* of the medicine men and how they are educated. They all have a most peculiar expression. They are hollow-eyed, but the pupil protrudes and rolls, and there is a keenness, a furtiveness, about them. Since the death of the boy referred to in a former letter, the medicine men have been doing their work with a will, but the event which they thus take advantage of has not been without good results. Had God restored to health and life everyone whom we've tried to help, we could hardly have convinced the people that we had no miraculous gift. More and more they would have pressed upon us and have professed faith for the sake of this material life. We foresaw something of this danger, this materializing of the spiritual. There are not nearly so many who now call upon God, but those who do seem to come up to a higher plane than before. They see something beyond this life.

In speaking of these medicine men, however, I must not omit one sign of hope for which we have

Shaman and Sick Man
(from S. Jackson, *Alaska*)

to be thankful. A daughter (four or five years of age) of him whom we consider the worst of the medicine men was born with curly hair. So of course she was destined to the medicine doctor's profession and her hair left uncut, uncombed, to become a matted mass like her father's, while she was adorned with necklace of teeth and charms of green stone. I so well remember the first time I saw her. It was on a Sabbath. She walked along from church just before us. Her beautiful child-face in the mass of unkempt hair struck me.

Some weeks ago that child came to church neat, clean, and that sacred mass of hair lay in smooth braids. So now she can never be a medicine woman.

DECEMBER 14

The Chilkats are the strongest people, and this district is the largest under the care of any missionary in Alaska. It is not one village, as is the case in the other stations, but four within a radius of thirty miles. We feel the urgent need of industries in which the people can engage. They are willing and eager, but we have little for them to do and little means to pay them. We hope fish canneries may be established on our rivers. These would furnish employment for many and thus provide them with a means of sustenance.

We expect and dread the coming of miners in the spring. Some prospectors took several hundred dollars' worth of gold down last fall, and we hear that many others are coming up. The mines at Juneau are about seventy-five miles below us.

About thirty thousand dollars' worth of gold dust was taken from there last season.

There is tillable land here, and we have perhaps an acre grubbed out where we hope to make a garden in the spring. We mean to try raising what's desirable, if seeds and slips come in time...

DECEMBER 28

Last Friday evening a rowboat arrived from Juneau with two naturalists from Berlin—Drs. Aurel and Arthur Krause—who intend to study here till spring, boarding at the trader's. They brought a package of mail, which they offered with evident pleasure for our Christmas gift. It proved to be Sitka mail for San Francisco, whither ours may have been sent by mistake. So we had no letters but had a pleasant Christmas with thoughts of the loved ones at home. I had work enough, you may be sure, in providing, from my brain, my wardrobe and my scrap bag, presents for sixty-nine school boys and girls and women. We graded them by number of days in attendance and had something for each one. The gentlemen brought cotton-jeans for pants for the boys.

The snow is waist deep on the men, who have to travel on snowshoes. Sabbath before last I went to meeting by a path walled with the crystal snow high as my head. It has snowed much since and snow lies piled up against our windows...

Carrie M. Willard

Chilkat Man Wearing a Buckskin Suit
Trimmed with Fur and Quills
The narrow snowshoe is used in hunting and running.
The broad snowshoe is used in packing.

CHILKAT MISSION MANSE
HAINES, ALASKA
JANUARY 23 & 30, 1882

TO THE SABBATH SCHOOL OF THE PRESBYTER-
IAN CHURCH OF EAST SPRINGFIELD, NEW YORK;
DEAR FRIENDS: The close of our third quarter in
Alaska finds us with not a few tokens of God's
pleasure in our work. We are more and more
enjoying it, and more and more its peculiarities
and needs open up to us. You have asked us to tell
you of these needs, and in this letter I will do so.

Do you remember on what a long, long day our
first letter was written you in June? Now we have
had the other extreme—a night long enough for
the littlest sleepyhead, the sun rising near eleven
a.m. and our lamps being lighted at three p.m.

During most of the winter thus far, the snow
has been about four feet deep. It is near six feet
now, yet the people go about easily on snowshoes
made of light, gracefully shaped wooden frames
woven across with thongs, exactly as cane is
woven into chairs at home. They are kept in place
on the foot by means of the strap which passes
from across the toes back and around the ankles.

Last Friday evening we were delighted by the
arrival of a canoe from Juneau bringing us precious letters written in October and November.

The canoe that brought the letters was that of
the parents of the girl whom Chief Don-a-wok
had been almost compelled to take for wife. It
came bringing him presents, but some time ago
the child had left his house and had gone to her
aunt's. We had a long talk with Don-a-wok before
she left. He said the child was unhappy, crying

continually, but that according to customs, he could not send her away. If her parents would take her back when they found how unhappy she was, he would be glad. However, she took the matter into her own hands and ran away.

When her parents learned this on arriving here, they were greatly mortified and incensed against Don-a-wok. They came to us before emptying their vials of wrath on their son-in-law, and God gave us such success with them that they seemed to see it all in a new light and gave up having a quarrel. I think they will take her back to Sitka and send her to school.

Mr. Willard returned a few days ago from a tour of the villages. Two weeks ago he started by canoe for Chilkoot, but got caught on the way in floating ice from the large glaciers. He and the man with him worked for their lives for an hour and the two were obliged to give up the journey. They turned into the fishing village of Tanani, and Mr. Willard came home the same evening.

But on the Chilkat River he was gone a little over a week, holding school in the upper villages. He went on snowshoes and skates. In the meantime I stayed here at home with just my baby Carrie and Kittie for company. I held daily court and the service on Sabbath. It occurred to me that to home friends it would seem startling if they knew that I sat night after night alone, the windows of the sitting room, without blinds, frequently revealing the faces of those who wished to come in. But then, as at all times here, there was a sweet and peculiar assurance of safety—no dread nor fear.

The greatest burden which falls upon me in my husband's absence is the care of the people—the responsibility of making decisions alone. With this people, among whom there are many complications of the family and tribal relations, together with ancient customs and superstitions, a small matter often becomes great in its consequences. We need more than man's wisdom.

We were besieged, as usual, for medicine and comforts for the sick. An old woman died and was cremated, whereupon Cla-not, the young second chief here, called the people together for a general peacemaking. On the Sabbath evening before Mr. Willard went away, he had spoken to the people about peace and brotherly love. Four years ago (though on the occasion of preaching that sermon he knew nothing of this bit of history), an old woman was charged with having bewitched a young man. Her son was so ashamed that he killed his mother. Custom required peace payment to be made for her murder to her brother, although it was he who accused her of witchcraft.

But payment had never been made, and the tribes became enemies within the same village, not entering each other's houses. While my husband was away, Cla-not, as I said, called these tribes together and reiterated this old story. He then said, "You all know what the minister talked to us about last Sunday. I have called you here to make that peace. We must make it tonight; we do not know what tonight or tomorrow may bring."— so nearly the scriptural phrase, though I think it had not been used in the sermon at all. Well, they made peace, Cla-not himself paying the blankets.

I had this good news to tell the missionary when he returned so weary that dark night from his long and difficult tramp through wind and rain and knee-deep slush.

He, in turn, had much to tell me of hard but joyful work, of the people's evident gladness at his coming, of how kindly they had treated him, and of his acquisition of several new Tlingit phrases, for he went without an interpreter. Four of the head men and several others came down with him to trade. Old Shat-e-ritch, the head chief, stayed with us. We invited them all to stay over Sabbath, and they gladly consented.

The night after they came down, Cla-not's peace was broken. He had insulted a powerful man of his tribe last fall, who then threatened to kill Cla-not but then repented. When Cla-not had inaugurated peacemaking, this man, Skookum (strong) Jim, bought white man's food at the store and called Cla-not to a feast of peace at which to pay blankets for his threat. Cla-not would not accept these overtures. Thus Cla-not's life was again threatened, and war seemed imminent. To make matters worse and the trouble general, Cla-not quarreled with his wives (who are mother and daughter), and they left his house. They are of the Sitka people, and if peace had not been restored before the arrival of the Sitka chief and the parents of Don-a-wok's wife, both of the same tribe as Cla-not's wives, (Don-o-wok being Cla-not's uncle), I fear we should not have been able to stay the flood. The complications were many and of such a character as would have involved the whole Chilkat country and the Sitka people.

This is an example of the sort of work we have here. We sent for Cla-not. He returned answer that he was busy. But late in the evening he came with a heavy expression on his blackened face. Shaking hands with him—against his will, apparently—we asked him to sit down, and Mr. Willard began to tell him of how Cla-not was the first Chilkat Mr. Willard had ever heard of, and that it was in answer to his request for a missionary that we came here. Mr. Willard told him how glad he had made us by his prompt peacemaking. Now we had heard he was in trouble and we had sent for him that we might know all the truth and be able to help him further. He was sullen at first, then full of anger at his enemy, but in the course of three hours' talk, he became very quiet, even though we gave him the gospel law in regard to wives as well as enemies. He had eaten nothing since his trouble began and refused to do so until the matter was settled in some way.

The second morning after, of his own accord he came in like a different man to tell us he had changed his mind and wished to have peace everywhere. His wives came back, and he made a great feast with Skookum Jim as chief guest.

Then the upper village people who were here had had some differences with this people, and they joined together for a big smoke. On Saturday night old Chief Shat-e-ritch told us that everybody was making peace and he wanted to do so too. He had one thing to settle in his own village, which he would do when he went back home.

On Sabbath morning you may be sure we had a grand peace meeting. The schoolhouse was

Chilkat Mother and Child Going to Church

crowded. In one space perhaps less than six feet square I counted twenty-eight persons. There would have been no room for benches if we'd had them. Even the old medicine men, who had not been at a meeting for weeks, were there. After service of two or three hours, we had a hasty lunch and went back. We had the children recite their catechism and about twenty verses of Scripture in both English and Tlingit, blending these with singing and prayer in both languages, and another sermon.

The upper village people were so impressed with the children's exercises that Shat-e-ritch made arrangements to have his son board at the trader's and attend school. Mr. Willard teaches English, and the whole congregation repeats the Lord's Prayer in concert every Sabbath in Tlingit.

We were very tired that evening and thought the people were too, but just before dark two of the head men came, begging us to have another meeting because they were going to the Stick country and it would be so long before they could come again. All the other people wanted another meeting too, they said. So, of course, we had the service. Mr. Willard gave them a basket of the living bread to take with them to the Stick country. This morning they left, and we are trying to get some mail ready to send with the next canoe.

Now I want to tell you about our schoolhouse. It is a rough up-and-down board shanty, sixteen by thirty feet. It may do for a schoolhouse for awhile, but a larger meeting house is a necessity. We shall soon be obliged either to have service out of doors or to turn away many who are anxious to hear the word of life. As it is now, the people average scarcely more than a square foot each in the space they occupy. They have been accustomed to huddling together in a way perfectly surprising to a white person, but they do not like it in church. They say now they do not wish to sit on the floor. Many stand through the service as close together as cord wood rather than sit down in such a mass on the floor.

We expect many more people in the spring. They are coming from above to build here. They ought to build the meeting house themselves, but they are not yet ready for that.

Mr. Willard thinks that we could build the best possible house for this locality, and at much less expense than a frame, out of the native forest which surrounds us here, fitting the logs into each other with moss. This could be done by the Indians at twenty-five cents per log, while white labor would cost three dollars and a half per day. It could give employment to the Native people, for which they are suffering. This matter gives us no little concern—how to employ people. They are waking up to new wants. They are rapidly becoming anxious to work that their wants may be supplied. That their wants should be supplied is necessary to the further growth and development of those whom we are trying to bring into the light.

There is another thing which grows upon us: the necessity of more special work for the children. Something must be done for these children. Dozens of these children have been brought to us by their parents, who begged us to take them and teach them. As we are situated, it is impossible to do this, however our hearts may yearn over them.

We had spoken with Dr. Sheldon Jackson about the natural advantages for a Home here, but he was burdened with personal obligations in getting the mission started at all, and he said, "No. There is a boys' Home at Sitka and a girls' Home at Fort Wrangell. Let them go *there*." So with might and main, when they come to us, we tell them of those Homes and beseech them to send their children there, but invariably come the impatient gathering up of the blanket, the averting of the head, and the decided "Clake," *no*.

They will not. Their tribal feeling is strong and pride in their own mission, to a degree, is proper and gratifying, and the truth is, after all, that though the Sitka Home is a desirable haven for Sitka boys, it can be filled from the lower coast. Further, it is not wholly desirable that our boys should go there.

And another thing: we are convinced that a Home here could become self-supporting in a very few years and perhaps support all this mission. We have an abundance of good soil—lying well, much of it—that would require almost no labor to prepare for cultivation. We could raise enough "truck" here to supply the whole coast, and our vegetables would find ready market and good prices at the mines. If we had a steam launch, we could control the whole matter with no middleman to eat up profits.

We believe that this would be a profitable investment for the work here that anyone could make—in *every sense* profitable, for we think that no other one thing could have such an influence on the people. The cost to begin with would be comparatively small. The house could be built of logs. We can have the land now for the taking, but if report is true, that will not be for long. A rush of population is predicted for Chilkat in the coming spring. We would require a good practical farmer and his wife to take charge of the Home and farm. The very first season the boys could provide their own vegetables and fish, and I believe we could fill such a Home in less than a week from our own villages. Will you not help us?

May God guide and bless us all...

Carrie M. Willard

CHILKAT MISSION
HAINES, ALASKA
FEBRUARY 3, 1882

TO THE LITTLE MISSION BAND OF THE SECOND PRESBYTERIAN CHURCH, NEW CASTLE, PENNSYLVANIA; MY DEAR FRIENDS: You cannot know just how much good it did us when we heard from one of your number these words: "We have a mission band now and are working for Alaska." You will have large rewards in your hearts now. When I heard that your hearts were turned toward this strange land, I wanted to tell you more about Alaska and will try to do so. Did you have a Thanksgiving day at home this year? We had one here on the third Thursday of November. The people had never heard of such a thing before, but for a week or two before, we talked with them about it so that when the day came they were ready.

Early in the morning our bright flag was up clear to the top of the pole, where the wind waved it joyously. The snow was white and deep and the day clear and beautiful. At about eleven o'clock the bell was rung, giving out its quickest, happiest tones. Almost at its first tap, the people poured into the schoolhouse. I wish you could have seen them as they answer such a summons—the eager, pleasant faces, the hurried steps of all, the moving and gorgeous colors of their clothing against the snow at their feet, and the bluish black of the pine forest around them, the great mountains behind and above all, the glassy waters of the bay giving back the shadows of the woods and colors of the sky. After they had sung and prayed and listened, the meeting closed and the playing began indoors and out. But the boys soon wearied of making snowmen as they became too much like Jack Frost's children themselves. In the evening we had the two best classes of the school come to a party in our home, which they seemed to enjoy very much.

Then I think you would like to hear about our Christmas. Just think! Sixty-nine children, besides some grown folks! It's good I have a long scrap bag because I had to use many a bit, and all my wit. Many of the children were irregular in attendance at school, so about two months before Christmas, I told them about it and that the presents would be graded according to their works. So I had to grade every child and present. Mrs. Dickinson, the teacher, knit several collars of yarn and two scarves and gave me about a dozen tiny dolls out of the store, which helped a good deal. Then Kittie dressed the dolls, and she and Mr. Willard trimmed the house with evergreens and flags. We had a splendid tree, too. For one of our head girls, I made a charming little hood out of an old red flannel pants leg and a bit of black velvet. For a good many others, I made little bags out of an old blue silk ruffle and filled them according to works with buttons, needles, thread and thimbles. For some, I made only red flannel needle leaves, and for others, handkerchiefs with the turkey-red initial of their English name.

To show you how such things are prized, I must tell you how a young woman was dressed the other day at church. She has beautiful, soft, shining hair, which waves back and hangs loose at her neck. Her eyes are large, dark and bright; her cheeks rosy. She wore a skirt of brilliant orange flannel and a loose blouse waist of a light, figured calico. About her neck was a white handkerchief over which was turned a narrow, bright blue ribbon, crossed in front and pinned with my scarlet, flannel needle leaves.

Generally, the people are fond of bright colors, but there are exceptions. On Sabbath I noticed a young woman who kept her eyes down and seemed to be troubled, so after service I spoke to Mrs. Dickinson about it. She said that I may have noticed the woman wore a new red blanket and had made the remark to the interpreter after church that she felt as though she was in everybody's eye. She never wore the blanket again.

The women are always modestly dressed. They have a long, loose gown of calico gathered to a yoke at the top; over this, a calico skirt. When dressed up, they have a jacket to match the skirt, a blanket around them and either a brightly colored cotton or a black silk handkerchief over their heads. Girls dress the same, only sometimes with moccasins or even leather knee-pants, but more often with no clothing for feet or legs. The men generally wear calico shirts and unbleached muslin drawers. They have moccasins, which they sometimes wear with high tops, sometimes lengthened into pants. They are large enough to admit of several folds of blanket, which takes the place of stockings. The boys, with few exceptions, wear nothing indoors. This custom is varied when they go to church by the addition of a calico shirt.

In the morning the men and boys go down to the water in the river, break a hole in the ice and dive into it. Then, coming out, they roll in the snow over and over and betake them to the house again. They think this makes them strong.

These people show the greatest family affection. In one case beautiful—a family of father and five girls, the baby just beginning to walk and the eldest about ten years. Their mother was shot last summer during the war in the upper village. The father and girls are here now, and I never saw more manifest love in any family.

Now before I close this already long letter, I must tell you an incident to show you how much some of these children appreciate their school. Before the people came here and built houses last fall, some of the children would bring a lunch of dried salmon on Saturdays and stay all week, sleeping in an outbuilding. At last came the great fish festival, the gayest time of all the year to the Indians, when they take their fish for winter and at nights have their mask dance with much music and feasting. The children went home for their food, and only one returned—faithful Willis of about ten years of age. We afterward heard the story from the village people. The good times proved too much for the other children, and they determined to stay and enjoy them.

It is for these little ones that you and we are working and for whom we long to have a refuge. If the miners come here in the spring, the evil influences will be greatly increased, and our girls especially will be the sufferers. We are thankful that God sent us here before the miners.

Carrie M. Willard

CHILKAT MISSION
HAINES, ALASKA
FEBRARY 17, 1882

MY DEAR FRIENDS: We held a regular council of war yesterday. A man named Sitka Jack had brought charges against one of the Chilkats for having killed, in Juneau last fall, Jack's wife, who was of his own tribe. Jack, being short of funds, was determined to have payment and was more than ready to fight for it. On the other hand, the accused denied the charge and demanded the proof, which Jack could not give.

We knew nothing of the trouble until about fifty of the men of both tribes filed into our house with their faces painted black and red and their heads tied up. They arranged themselves—one tribe in a close row on one side of the room, the other tribe on the opposite side—and called for the minister. I had dinner just ready to put on the table, but I set it back and called Mr. Willard from the study. That was the last of dinner till about eight o'clock that evening. We had no interpreter but Kittie. The poor child did grandly in the circumstances, which were of a trying nature to all.

Hour after hour the loud charges were made and the refutation as loudly and angrily given, until we were all tired out. Mr. Willard, after getting the run of the trouble, took paper and pencil and, charging the men to tell the whole truth and nothing else, he proceeded to write down their words for the man-of-war, to which he referred the whole matter. Several times they seemed on the very point of breaking over into cutting and shooting. Twice in particular I thought it was come to that, but while I held Baby tightly in my arms, Mr. Willard had sprung into the middle of the floor and with a tremendous setting down of his feet and bringing down of his fist, and with a voice that almost made me quail, he brought them back to something like order.

Then he stood up and talked to them till you could hear a pin drop, except for the oft repeated "Yug-geh" (good). Old Jack left with angry threats before the good feeling came, when he found that he could gain nothing unjustly through us.

We had a delightful gathering of the children tonight. All seemed to have a nice time, and we feel it must have done good. We made Willis master of ceremonies, and all did so well. After leaving their kerchiefs and blankets in the public room, they came to the sitting room to shake hands with us. We told them each, in their own language, that we were glad to see them. There must have been over a hundred of them. We played many games, sang, talked and prayed together, and then said good-night.

The Stick Indians of the interior, from whom our people get their furs, are a simple and, as far as we can judge, honest tribe. The Chilkats, to prevent the Sticks' coming to the coast to trade, have told the Sticks horrid stories of the whites, and that the Sticks would be killed if they came. The few who have ventured here have been

dogged about by the Chilkats. We have, neverthe-
less, gotten hold of every one for a talk.

One of the Sticks brought a nice squirrel robe
to Mr. Willard last week, and as Mr. Willard
wanted one, he bought it at just the same price
that he would pay either a Chilkat or the trader.
Mr. Willard paid in flour, shot and powder.

You can scarcely imagine the hornets' nest
that was stirred up. The people were ready to
mob us. Early next morning, before we could get
our breakfast, we were set upon by some of the
head men, of whom Cla-not was spokesman.
Many and many a time he had asked prices of
goods, and we had told him. But he wanted us to
tell him the truth and everybody else a lie. He
charged us with having robbed the Chilkats, for,
said he, "The Sticks are our money. We and our
fathers before us have gotten rich from them.
Now you have taken away our riches."

Mr. Willard told him that he'd spoken the
truth to all men nor would he lie for any. He told
him that a certain advance on prices here was
just and right when they carried their goods into
the interior, but that it was wrong to hinder the
Sticks from coming here. Mr. Willard said that
when the Sticks brought their skins here, it was
only right that they should buy and sell at the
same prices which the Chilkats did. He asked the
head men what they brought into this world and
what they expect to take out of it and tried to
show them that they were heaping up wrath
against the day of wrath.

That one question as to his natural prestige,
although Mr. Willard has used it many times to

check their pride, seemed altogether new to Clanot and touched him more than anything else. Clanot reminded us of his high class and that his father and grandfather had had wealth before him. He told us that he had come to this place expecting us to build him a house, as the missionary had in Fort Simpson. There the people prayed and then told the missionary, and he gave them what they asked for. The people here, he said, could not believe what we preached to them, then gave them nothing, and now we had taken away what they had. He would stay in this place no longer. He has not allowed his wife to come to church since we talked to him here about polygamy. He says if he lets her hear, she will give him shame—leave him, I suppose he means. He has three wives.

You must not for one moment imagine from anything written here that we are weary of our work or ready to give it up, or discouraged, for such a thought would be far from the truth. We expected trials. It was from no momentary enthusiasm or impulse that we entered upon this work. Our minds have never wavered for an instant. Our expectations have been realized—not just in the way we looked for, perhaps, but in trials greater than we could have known. Yet we have reason to rejoice and be exceedingly glad.

FEBRARY 20

On Saturday we came home from our usual visiting of the village with sick hearts, having been confronted with the charge that we had brought on this terrible winter of storm and snow. First it was because those children had been buried instead of cremated. Then Mr. Willard had put on his snowshoes in the house. And last, we had allowed the children that night in their play to imitate the noise of a wild goose.

We had few at church yesterday, and those mostly children. We did not know the reason until this morning. Two women came to us in great trouble. One, the mother of the first child that was buried, had been the subject of persecution for some time, and now, since Jack had gone below and Cla-not was away seal hunting, the people declared that should the storm continue and the canoes be lost, they would kill her. All day Sabbath the people had been ready to kill her. She had slept none that night.

The people were out of food and were unable on account of the snow to go to their village store houses for more. They were desperate. If she did not get the minister to show her where the grave was and build a fire over it, they would kill her. The women said the people had built great fires over the other little graves and had brought two days of beautiful weather. Mr. Willard told the women that neither the burial nor the place had been a secret. It had been done in daylight. All had the opportunity of knowing all about it. Then we talked with the two women for a long time. They listened so well that they went away saying the people might do what they like, but no fire would be built.

FEBRUARY 23

The storm continuing, the mother yielded. This morning there is a great fire on the beach.

The fall has been indeed exceptional. I am sure we must have had twenty-five feet of snow at least. It thaws and sinks so that it has hardly exceeded eight feet in depth at any time, and it is so solid that one can walk over it anywhere. But the storms are sometimes so blinding that traveling is next to impossible. Our house is built high, yet as I look out of the window, I see only the snow-covered apex of the outbuilding roofs and a few treetops. The mountains are entirely lost in the storm, and the waters of the bay are far below my snow wall.

A man wanted to cut some wood for us last week, and he dug out the cord. You should see the cavern—down, down, so far beneath the surface. But a different picture our interior presents, with its brightly carpeted sitting room, roaring wood fire, big windows of light, and the green trailing moss on pictures and walls, and table and shelf of brightly covered books from friends. As one of the Indians said to me one evening when, unable to go to church, I sat reading at home, "You can stay here all alone and yet have many friends, for your books talk to you like people." Do you not think that was a bright remark? Above all, our home is bright because of its quiet content and its little white bird in the blue gingham apron, whose music grows sweeter every day. I wish I could give you a correct likeness of her.

FEBRUARY 27

No hint of outbuildings now, and even by mounting a chair, I cannot see over the snow against the window. We had only about sixty at church yesterday. The women were out in a body, working nearly all day at the snow with their canoe paddles, trying to find a grave, with no success. Late last evening the women came again to get Mr. Willard to go with them. Of course he would not go. This morning before breakfast, our kitchen was filled with them again. He told them that he knew no more about the grave than they did. If he did, he would not show them, and he wished them to come no more for such a purpose.

Another fire was kindled on the beach last week for burning the hair of a girl who'd combed it outside the house. It was cut close to her head and burned to avert catastrophe.

Let me tell you of another of the people's practices. When a girl is twelve or fourteen years old, she is secluded for a length of time great in porportion to her caste—from six months to two years—in a little dark room. During this time she is not allowed to see the daylight nor any face save her mother's, who, when necessary, goes out with the girl after nightfall, and then the latter is closely blanketed.

Some evenings ago a father and mother brought their daughter to me in great distress. The people were angry because she was not secluded according to custom and it was not safe for her to be seen alone. The medicine men declared that this was one cause of the great snowstorm. We had a long talk with these parents. The father said that to show me how the people believed these things, he would tell me what was done before we came. He told us that a girl of high class during a time of bad weather was the subject of this charge by the medicine men. She denied it. The storm continued. They told her that if she did not confess it, they would kill her. They then commenced to torture her by burning her blanket from her by inches to extort her confession. Her blanket was half burned from her body. Still she denied. Still the storm raged. They next killed a slave, but without the desired effect on the girl. Last of all they killed her and burned her body, whereupon immediately the storm abated and they had beautiful weather. When told that these customs were not heeded by the Fort Wrangell Indians, and that they did not have storms as a result, the parents quickly replied that this country was different. The least thing could bring snow here. We tried to explain to them how and why it was different.

March has come in like a lamb. Last evening we saw the sun set gloriously after so long, and this morning it rose with equal splendor. About noon we heard the report that the women had at last been successful in finding the grave sometime during the forenoon.

MARCH 25

Just after I wrote you last our trials in sickness began, but God has brought us through!

Our little Carrie was taken with I know not what. She chilled and fretted and cried, had no appetite, yet seemed to be starving, and seemed to have a severe head cold. We got no rest. At length, on Saturday night, among other ways of soothing her, I tried rubbing her back with my bare hand and found to my astonishment (for she had so long been exposed to it without having taken the disease), that smallpox was coming out.

In the early morning, I called Mr. Willard to make the fires and put water on to pack Baby, for she was cold. The smallpox was not coming out well. He was not feeling good either, having his first old-fashioned headache since coming here. Upon getting up, he almost fainted. At last, after lying down between attempts to dress himself (Baby meanwhile screaming), he got out to the sitting room, called Kittie, and got a fire made.

As soon as possible I got little Carrie into a soda water pack, which quickly soothed her so much that she allowed Kittie to hold her while I attended to Mr. Willard, who by this time was rolling on the floor in his misery. Having bathed his head, got his feet to heating, and making him a cup of tea, which he could not swallow, I drank a mouthful myself and took our fretting child. After an hour or so I got her down in a sweet sleep of two hours, still in the pack. Then I found Mr. Willard almost delirious. He did not know what ailed him but complained of agonizing pain and of burning up, although his skin felt cold and clammy, and his color was a mixture of purple, white, and green. I soon had a cot up in the sitting room, kettles of boiling water, tub, wringer and blankets, and fairly forced the almost crazy man into a scalding pack with flatirons all around. I dispatched Kittie to Mrs. Dickinson to tell her of our situation and that I wished she would hold the Sunday school.

Mr. Willard grew alarmingly ill. Baby woke crying. I took her out of her three-and-a-half hours' pack and gave her a bath. She was then brighter and better, the smallpox out pretty well. Then I went back to Mr. Willard. Kittie stayed hour after hour. Not another soul came near. At last he fell asleep, and by and by my anxious eyes saw that the sleep grew natural, and a better color came into his face. After about two hours there came a little natural perspiration, and when I took him out, although he was weak as a child, he was himself again. In the course of a week. He had almost regained his old footing.

Little Carrie soon became very restless again. The irritation was fearful. The immense pocks had pits of white matter as large as peas, and on a part of her body so thick that I could not lay a finger tip between them. Fortunately there were none on her face or hands, though they were thick on her head. I packed her again, and at bed-time bathed her with weak saltwater. Still there was no rest with all I must do for several days and nights, though she was doing well and in two weeks had entirely recovered. The Indians are sick with the disease many weeks, sometimes months, and quite a number have died.

Of course after this siege, I did not feel quite young, but I was happy in having my dear ones living and well, and you know as well as I that I had, in turn, the tenderest care and nursing when I needed it....

Carrie M. Willard

CHILKAT MISSION
HAINES, ALASKA
APRIL 5, 1882

REV. SHELDON JACKSON, DEAR BROTHER: The *Favorite* came in yesterday afternoon with mail from the middle of November up to March. Of course it took us till midnight to look it over, read and arrange, and then we retired before we were through but not to get one wink of sleep.

We received a flag by express and our piano. The latter is in the sitting room. I have already played some old tunes for the Indians. I think playing it did me more good than them, though they were delighted. The piano came without a case from Sitka, as it alone had barely been rescued by the miners from the fires which utterly destroyed the boys' Home and much of their goods. The fire left Mr. and Mrs. Austin homeless and impoverished again. Oh, I long to give them everything I have! What trials they have had! And how nobly they bear them!

What a mingling of feelings these letters give us—so much of sorrow and yet so much of joy.

Our village here will soon be left to itself. The Indians are even now commencing to separate. Some go to the lower Chilkat, some to Chilkoot, and some to Tanani, a fishing village between this and Chilkoot, about three or four miles by water from here. Others go up the Taiya Inlet some fifteen miles and others to the upper village; so that Mr. Willard's circuit-riding—or, rather, paddling—will soon commence.

Carrie M. Willard

DEAR FRIENDS: The Sunday school papers are indeed a treasure. We have had none for a good while, and the people seem hungry for them. I never saw such eagerness at Christmas as these people evinced, old and young, as the papers came out. The papers are hoarded as a great treasure, the pictures pored over right side up, upside down and sideways. The school children pick out the little words and enjoy that.

You ask about the animals here. Cinnamon, black and brown bears are said by the Indians to be numerous in the woods all around us. In crossing the trail to the lower villages the men always carry knives or guns with them. Foxes, wolves, wolverines and many other animals abound. There are many reindeer [caribou] farther in the interior. We have many varieties of birds. I have seen more eagles, ravens and gulls than any other birds, but there are grouse of different kinds, the most beautiful being the snow-white [ptarmigan]. In the waters there are seals, walruses and beaver; halibut and spotted, red, and white salmon; a delicious little silver fish, in size and shape resembling the small herring. These latter are the fish which the people are said to use for candles, sticking the head in the ground and lighting the tail. They also make of them a grease white as lard, which they prize for food. Ducks are plentiful, from the mallard down to the small fish-duck, but we do not get many of them.

One day I saw that a man had brought in a young seal. I went down to the boat where he and his wife were unloading and told him I wished to buy a piece. The woman shook her head, saying that seal meat would make white people sick. I insisted, and at length had the satisfaction of seeing the animal skinned and quartered. Under the skin there is a layer of pure fat from one to two inches thick all over the animal. This is used for oil. The flesh is almost black. For bones, there are but the backbone and ribs. I baked my purchase for dinner. It was not bad, nor can I say that we liked it much. The taste is a cross between fish and mammal.

As I mentioned, there have been two brothers here in the Chilkat country since Christmas, by the names of Aurel and Arthur Krause, both doctors of natural science from the University of Berlin, Prussia. They consider this country rich, and in scenery they say it surpasses everything they ever saw before, although they have spent months among the Alps and have traveled extensively through the East. They crossed the American continent—last spring, I think—and went on a whaler to Siberia, where they remained some months before coming here. They are indefatigable workers and have quite upset the old geography of this locality, making a new map of it. I asked Dr. Arthur (the elder brother left for home by the last steamer) if their reports had been printed in America. He said only a few geographical items: the rest were sent directly to Germany with innumerable specimens...

Carrie M. Willard

TO THE SABBATH SCHOOL OF THE PRESBYTER
IAN CHURCH OF EAST SPRINGFIELD, NEW YORK, MY
DEAR FRIENDS: The steamer *Favorite* dropped
into our harbor on Tuesday of last week for the
first time since last October, and we do not expect
to see her again before the autumn. Thus our
dependence will be upon chance canoes for mail
and supplies for another six months.

I have been questioned in regard to facilities
for communication with the outer world. They are
meagre. Port Townsend, in Washington Territory,
is the most northwesterly port in the United
States. Vessels are frequent between that point
and San Francisco and Portland. Also a railroad,
connecting by stage with the Central Pacific, runs
to within a few miles of Port Townsend. From
that point there is but one steamer per month
that leaves for the north, or aims to do so, on the
first day of each month. If a letter is an hour
behind the leaving of the steamer, it will be a
month late in reaching any Alaskan port. Also, if
that letter misses our semi-annual steamer at
Juneau and no chance canoe comes along bound
for the Chilkat country, it may be six months late
in reaching us. The steamer from Port Townsend
touches first at Fort Wrangell, then Sitka, then
Juneau, and goes back by way of Fort Wrangell.

The *Favorite* is a small trading vessel which
merely runs between the Alaskan posts of the
North-West Trading Company as their stores
demand new supplies or have a quantity of furs

to send below. Last summer the *Favorite* visited this point several times, but hereafter, I believe, they expect to make the trip only in spring and fall. It is the only steamer which comes nearer than Juneau, except as occasion demands the presence of the man-of-war anchoring at Sitka.

You wish to know what we have to eat and where it comes from. Of course, this first year we have no food except as we buy it. What you buy "downtown," we order from Portland or San Francisco, from fifteen hundred to two thousand miles away. If our goods are left behind, as they were last fall, we are brought to great want or to the unpleasant alternative of purchasing inferior store goods at high rates. Owing to a repugnance of doing this, both because of the lead distress which the poor canned goods gave us and because we dreaded being in debt, we have frequently tried the former plan. We have always had flour, and I have learned how to make many dishes out of bread, in lieu of meat, vegetables and fruit. Occasionally we have been fortunate enough to get beautiful spotted trout from the river at the upper village, and now and then ducks, Indian chickens and grouse. But on account of the great snow the people have lain almost dormant so far as hunting is concerned.

In summer both fish and berries are abundant, and of both there are many varieties. The former range from halibut to the small rock fish and from both salt and fresh water. We ate of eleven kinds of berries last summer, and still there were others we did not taste. We could, however, not often get more than enough for one meal at a time. We find the gooseberry, black currant, huckleberry and soft red raspberry of the States growing wild. The other varieties, so far as I know, are peculiar to this country.

The delicious trout are abundant through the winter in upper Chilcat River, the only difficulty being to get them brought down here. The men and boys catch them by cutting a hole in the ice and dropping in bait of salmon eggs, for which the trout come in great numbers. Then, with a peculiar sort of spear hook, the trout are brought up—as many as five at a time on one stick. But the people depend principally upon the salmon, which they dry during the month of September, and the salmon eggs and the salmonberry, which they preserve together in salmon oil. They prepare huckleberries for winter use, too, by washing them and drying them between two boards perhaps a foot square. The berry cake is about three-fourths of an inch thick, tart and tastes very strong of wood smoke. They also dry seaweed and use it with a general boiled dinner of salmon eggs, berries and oil in the same pot. The seaweed has certain medicinal properties which render it exceedingly valuable in such a bill of fare—much as our good and wise mothers at home value onions for their families. When this pot dinner is cooked, the pot itself is taken down from the hook and chain by which it is suspended from the roof beams over the great central fire, and the family gather about it with bone and wooden spoons varying in size according to the size of the individual. That belonging to the baby is about the size of a common soup ladle, while that used by the head of the household is near the size of his own head. When they do not boil their fish, they roast it. After splitting it open quite flat, they pass a little rod through it, crosswise at the top and bottom, and lengthwise a stick long enough to run into the ground and at the same time support the fish against the blaze.

You also inquire as to our fuel. It is wood alone, which in this part of the peninsula is abundant. So far we have seen no indications of coal among these mountains.

Now that the days are growing longer and warmer, it is a trying matter to walk without snowshoes, for in spots the snow has softened enough to suddenly let one down to the shoulders. This snow has been troublesome in terms of our trying to maintain interactions with the people.

At times through the winter it seemed doubtful whether we should see the spring, so intense would be the excitement of the people upon a return of the snows. At none of their old villages do they have anything to compare with the quantity of snows here. This difference is explainable to persons schooled in meteorology. The effect of the warm Japan current gives to Sitka a moist and agreeable climate. There is from this stream a great and constant evaporation, which in summer falls as rain among the mountains of that lower coast. During winter the course of winds is northward, and they bear with them these heavy vapors, which, as they come in contact with our mountains, are condensed and fall in the form of snow. If you examine the map of this country, you will see that Lynn Canal is walled by mountains, which at the head of the canal separate, admitting the Chilkoot and Chilkat Rivers. Between these rivers, with their farther mountain walls, is the Chilkat Peninsula, which, southward from our bay, is comparatively flat. Immediately at the head of the bay begins a mountain which extends unbroken across the peninsula, forming a perfect "back-step" and condenser to these burdened winds from the south.

Our mission lies in the lap of these mountains, her feet dropping into the bay, while the other villages lie to the north, under the sheltering shadow of these "everlasting hills." They are also protected by abrupt turns in the rivers. This explanation, natural to us, is beyond the comprehension of the people here, who have not been schooled in meteorology, and who are steeped in superstitions about the causes of weather.

Today, the 17th, the snow falls heavily, and I presume someone will take me to account for daring to bring into the house on my foot yesterday one of my snowshoes, which I could not readily remove. Another complaint was that the minister had made star figures on the snow during an outdoor lesson on astronomy and so brought bad weather. Upon several occasions we were taken by force, the people filing in until our room was filled. They came before breakfast, in the night and at all hours intervening. We tried reasoning, then ridicule, and lastly authority, forbidding them to trouble us any more with complaints or threats. Soon spring will be here, and their trouble on this score will be at an end. We pray ere next winter the light will have entered their hearts.

The Indians call us "the snow people"—not because they think we brought the snow, but because we are white. Baby Carrie they call "little snow woman." Mr. Willard they have named *Don-a-wok*, which means "silver eye" or "bright eye"...

Carrie M. Willard

CHILKAT MISSION
HAINES, ALASKA
MAY 8, 1882

MY DEAR MRS. HAINES: I have not yet heard from Mrs. Downing, but have taken the girl to do for her all in my power. It was a burden at this time, for my hands are full to overflowing; but I felt that taking her was the ordering of God, and that he would strengthen me for each task he gave.

A week ago last Saturday, April 29th, we found that our village here was almost deserted. The people had gone to Nauk Bay, ten or twelve miles down the channel, to fish. There is there an immense run of herring. Accordingly, we put our things together and followed the people to spend the Sabbath at their fishing ground. Some half dozen persons who had intended remaining here till Monday went down also on Saturday, as they said they could have no Sunday here without us. So there were left in this village only a few old people and some children, among them my Indian girl Fanny and her grandparents. They came down to Nauk on Sabbath just in time for church. Some of the people were glad to see us, but many looked dark at our coming. They had intended to work all that day.

MR. EUGENE WILLARD
CHILKAT MISSION
HAINES, ALASKA
APRIL 14, 1882

DEAR DR. JACKSON: If Mr. De Groff cannot succeed in sending our things that are in Juneau, I will try to go myself. The *Favorite* brought only flour enough for the trader and no potatoes, no bacon or other supplies. Moreover, the boat will not return before fall...

We have had Indian Lot of Wrangell with us for nearly a week. We were glad to have someone who could speak and lead in prayer. He intends to go on Monday. I bought from him about one bushel of potatoes for five dollars.

Chief Shat-e-ritch sends a letter to his son at Forest Grove. He says, "We are so far from the mission that we do not go every day to church, but we will go in the summer. Learn all you can. I do not want you to learn only one-half; learn all. When you are in the school, don't play, but study."

You will probably remember the deaf mute boy whom you hired to work on the house. We have discovered that by putting my watch in his mouth he can hear the singing. He never is absent from church or prayer meeting. I have thought that perhaps some Christian at home would like to give him an opportunity of hearing the words of life by providing him with a dentaphone.

Among our people there are three deaf persons who can all hear a loud sound, though it is impossible to hold a conversation with them. There is but one who cannot speak.

Eugene S. Willard

On Saturday we watched the people fishing. In the stern of the canoe sat a woman or child to paddle. In the prow stood a man with a long pole through which were driven many sharpened nails. This pole was used much in the same way as a paddle, but with every dip one to six fish were brought up and dropped into the canoe. In a short time the canoes were half filled and then taken ashore, and the fish emptied into great basins dug in the pebbly beach. There the women cleaned them and strung them on long sticks to dry. As the tide went out, children ran along the shore and gathered fish by the tubful from among the sea moss. The people worked late on Saturday night. We had our evening worship with a few of the children on the rocks overhanging the workers, who could hear the hymn.

At the dawn of Sabbath, six or eight canoes dropped down into the bay again for fish, but the parties soon returned with empty boats and long faces. Of course it was the missionary who had driven away the fish—all gone. There were still many fish undressed from the day before, and soon the camp presented as lively an appearance as on that day. The people were angry about the fish but set about building drying booths, whittling fish sticks, cleaning fish, etc.

My husband had hoisted the flag at worship time on Saturday evening, and at church time on Sabbath morning we took our seats on the rock beneath it and sadly looked on at the busy hands and sullen faces of the multitude below. A few of the school children who were allowed to do so washed the black paint from their faces and came to us. We then went down and made our way into the midst of the busy crowd of people, and Mr. Willard, taking a tin pan, drummed for them to stop work. A few did so and gathered closer around us. The others could not but hear as they worked, and others came to the afternoon service.

After church I noticed that Fanny had been set to work on the fish. I knew that she was working against her conscience, so I called her to come to me. I was impressed with the idea that if we were to save her, now was the time for a decisive step. After consulting together, Mr. Willard and I took her at once.

On Monday we brought her home with us. I put her into a tub of warm water and scrubbed her. Then braiding her long soft hair, I put her first into a clean nightdress and then into a clean bed. When I left her, after a bedtime talk and prayer and a goodnight kiss, I could but trust that the good Father had planned a noble future for this one whom he seemed to have given to us.

During the week, though it had seemed so full before that I could not get anything more into it, I managed to make Fanny an outfit—underclothes, skirt-dress, deerskin shoes, and stockings. She is only one of the many bright girls here whom I am besought to take into our home and for whom my heart longs and aches. But this poor body of mine!

Oh, Mrs. Haines, we must have a Home here, for these children must be saved, and it cannot be done in their homes. The idea for a Home has been growing upon us ever since we came here, but each day the necessity is more apparent, each day the burden is heavier on our hearts.

I did not speak to you of this before because I knew that the Board was burdened with work. I have had dozens of boys and girls brought to me by their parents, who beg me to take the children and teach them.

Carrie M. Willard

MR. EUGENE WILLARD
CHILKAT MISSION
HAINES, ALASKA
MAY 9, 1882

DEAR DR. JACKSON: I have had several talks with different Indians about taking mail to Juneau. They will not go for less than thirty dollars per month. Some want forty. They say they will need a large Hydah canoe and have at least three men in it. If there is any kind of a sea on, they cannot move with the canoes.

MAY 12

I did not succeed in sending the mail. It got as far as the middle of the bay, when the Indians said that some of the letters were sent to the storekeepers to tell them what the prices of skins were; so back came the mail. But this afternoon the *Favorite* blew her whistle in our harbor, and by her I can send to Sitka. She did not stop at Juneau. Therefore our incoming mail is not here and our freight is still in the warehouse there.

My traveling has commenced, as the Indians are away fishing. On the 30th of April we camped among the Indians about ten miles down the coast. There was at that time a depth of four or five feet of snow on the ground. At present

---

there is about one foot. I used a tin pan for a bell and a fine gravel beach for a meeting house. Don-a-wok's canoe and tent were secured, so we were comparatively comfortable.

I would like to go up the Taiya Inlet, where all the people of the village are fishing, but have no way of getting there. I do not like these good-for-nothing canoes. You must sit just so, look just so, and breathe just so, or over they go.

I was visited the other evening by the old Crow chief who gave us the house at the upper village. He said he wanted me to take his words and send them to the officers, telling them to have pity on those Indians who want to live in peace, adding, "And do not let the people buy molasses; it is no good." Another man said to me, "I don't understand why all people don't talk the same language." He wanted to learn to be a Christian.

MAY 24

I have never before appreciated our utter helplessness. Mrs. Willard has been sick for two weeks, with medicines no nearer than Juneau.

The Native teachers for the upper village, Louis and Tillie, have been with us one week. We were unable to procure a canoe to take them upriver to their station, as all the Indians are away fishing. We were glad to welcome them and took them into our house, at the same time telling them we could not do for them as we would if Mrs. Willard were well. We told them that until she was able to walk they should help themselves to our stove and stores.

Mrs. Willard's sickness was of such dangerous character as to require constant attention day and night. But I hope a turning point has been reached and she will soon be in her usual health.

We have had fine weather for weeks back, and now the snow has gone. We have radishes, onions, lettuce, beets, cabbage and tomato plants growing in boxes, waiting until I can get the ground broken. I hope to have plenty of vegetables for next year.

I have concluded to build a small log house for the teachers at the upper village, for the following three reasons: 1. Increasing complications in regard to the ownership and disposal of the proffered Indian house, and on this account the inadvisability of putting much expense on it; 2. There is no lumber here to fix it with; 3. Louis being able to get out shakes for a roof, I will be enabled to build a comfortable log dwelling at less expense.

JUNE 1

Again we were favored by the arrival of a canoe from Juneau, bringing some of our letters. We were rejoiced to see your letter, as always.

We were enabled to send Louis and Tillie to the upper village on Saturday. They will fix themselves up as comfortably as possible in the large house until I can get some way to send them more comfortable things. Having left their cookstove at Juneau, they must camp until it is sent up. I told Louis to start a garden, and while his food is growing he can work on the house.

Our people are still fishing, and we have but two scholars—one the faithful Willis. It will not be long, however, before the children will return, as the small fish are leaving.

No, we have not been burned out nor removed by tornado. We've been rocked by an earthquake.

The house was lightly jarred by the breaking of a glacier on the Shooting Mountain, on the Chilkat side above the Davidson Glacier.

JUNE 11

I am unable to finish as I wanted to do. A canoe goes to Juneau today. I can manage to get from one room to another and that is about all I can do. I have now been sick for over a week. My right hand and arm are swollen to twice the natural size. Mrs. Willard is a little better.

Your brother in Christ,
Eugene S. Willard

MRS. EUGENE WILLARD
CHILKAT MISSION MANSE
HAINES, ALASKA
JUNE 29, 1882

REV. SHELDON JACKSON, D.D., DEAR BROTHER: We are still prisoners, but I rejoice to say that I have the use of my hands—at least for awhile at a time. My husband can walk again, though slowly and feebly. It has been indeed a dark time. For many days we thought the end had come for us.

Before I was able to move myself, Mr. Willard hurt his hand digging in the garden. The hand at once took such a malignant form that it seemed beyond all human means, at least in this country, to save his life. We gave up hope but not effort, faith, and prayer.

While we both lay prostrate our only aid—the ten-year-old Indian girl Fanny—was taken with scarlet fever, and in a few days after, our baby Carrie also. To save her life we had to exert all our strength and skill. My arms were made strong to hold, bathe and pack her. Her father drew us with one hand from the bed to the stove on a rocking-chair. We had been unable to get ourselves any warm, good food for so long that I think we should at last have perished altogether if Mr. and Mrs. Dickinson had not come to our aid and offered us Jack long enough to cook us something each day. When Jack left after a few days, Mr. Dickinson kindly finished the week cooking for us himself. The children are both nearly well now, and we are all gaining. God has blessed us.

Mr. Willard had intended going to the upper village today, taking a man with him, for he is desperate. But Louis and Tillie came down today, very blue and homesick, I fear, though they are well and have had plenty to do. Their school even now numbers between fifty and sixty. They have put in a garden. Mr. Willard had told Louis to get out his shingles and logs as fast as he could, but of this latter work I believe he has done nothing.

The Indians have taken possession of the large house given to the mission and are going to tear it down to build up new as a monument to the dead. Shat-e-ritch has told us repeatedly that it will then be the mission house. But it seems that he has nothing whatever to say about it, and the other Indians say that when it is finished they will have rent for it.

But how are we to get anything from Juneau? We must have a boat of our own. We have had no freight since last fall, except our piano. The *Favorite* brought us not even a letter last time. Our potatoes and other provisions have been lying so long in the warehouse there that I suppose by this time they are past use, while we suffer for want of them and pay high rates of storage. It drives my husband almost wild, especially since he cannot work. He paces the floor, and I scarcely know whether he has greater distress of mind or body. He says he "may as well be locked up in a box." But "No, no!" I tell him. "It is not so bad, because we are free to teach Christ to these people. They cannot shut our mouths as long as the spirit is kept in our bodies, and you know we expected trials." We have not been able to get a canoe at any price, even when we were dying, as we thought, for medicine which may have been had only seventy-five miles away. Fish in their season mean more to the Indians than anything else, and all are using their boats for fishing.

We feel a good deal "cast down," you see, but oh, not in despair. God will take care of his work here. We are not necessary to its success. If we should not be spared to do it, I will believe that it is because someone else can carry it on better. But, oh, how I thank him for the privilege of doing at least one year's hard work in Chilkat!

I want to tell you that I do sometimes feel as though my course were almost run. If it should be and I am not permitted to write you again, I want to give you these words: Please do not feel, nor allow the Board to feel that they made a mistake in sending us, even though it was but for a year or two. God sent us here, and when he calls us away, our special work will be done, however imperfectly. Would that I might see the Church and Home here and, more than all, some fruit of souls saved! But I know that all will be well.

Though our path has led toward the valley of shadows, yet the days have been long and bright. On June 21st the sun rose at 2:45 a.m., setting at 9:15 p.m. The darkest hour was like early twilight, so that "even the night is light about us."

Carrie M. Willard

CHILKAT MISSION
HAINES, ALASKA
JULY 18, 1882

TO THE PRESBYTERIAN SABBATH SCHOOL OF EAST SPRINGFIELD, NEW YORK, MY DEAR FRIENDS: Since last quarter God has been giving us very different work from that of previous times, calling us to bear instead of to do, and I have been wondering whether or not I should let you see the missionary's cloud-land as well as his castles.

You know Jesus said, "Take up your cross and follow me." We did not leave ours in Pennsylvania when we came as missionaries to this remote place where there are neither doctors, nurses, nor medicines. We have all been very sick, near unto death, down among those shadows where my husband, little Carrie and I traveled together, yet apart. Precious to us proved the Master's words, "I am with you..."

Willard

If I am unable to send you a full and satisfactory letter this time, you will now understand why and excuse me. I have not gained good physical strength, and my husband is disabled from writing or in any way using his right hand. It still requires much attention and is painful.

Our people, so impatient of the long winter and needed food, lost no time in getting to their old haunts as soon as the small fish began to run in April. We had long hoped to be the possessors of some sort of a boat in time to enable us to begin touring when the people did. This hope not being realized, we were fortunate enough to secure passage on the last Saturday in April in Chief Don-a-wok's canoe, bound for Nauk Bay, wither the people had gone that week for herring.

Leaving here, as we did, with the ground still covered with snow and no sign of spring, we were surprised to find there not more than a foot of snow and in many places none at all. Instead we found tiny wild plants and blossoms growing. I wish I could show you just how beautiful it looked. We came first upon the bay where the people were tented near the shore in shelters made of fir and spruce boughs, with here and there a sailcloth hung in fantastic fashion. More important to the Indians than these were the fish frames upon which were already hanging the herring by hundreds of dozens, drying in the sun. These frames were erected upon the verge of the dark green wood, above and beyond which rose the snow-topped mountains, while immediately in front sloped the clean gravel beach to the glassy surface that was alive with canoes.

This nook one comes upon suddenly, so hidden is it in approaching by high, precipitous rocks covered with a wild growth of pine. Here on the rocks, among the sighing trees and overhanging the busy camp on the beach, we pitched our mission tent, intent on fishing too—for souls.

As we entered, the bay lay in profound silence except for the splashing of waterfalls among the rocks, the dipping of our own paddles, the startled cry of eagles and the screeches of seagulls, the number of which I have never seen equaled. They filled the air and covered the water like monstrous flakes in a heavy snowstorm.

This has been our only Sabbath out all summer so far, for after that Don-a-wok did not come back, and there was neither boat nor man to be hired. Soon after, our Native teachers, Tillie and Louis Paul, from the McFarland Home at Fort Wrangell, came to take charge of a school in the upper village. We were eager to get the work started there, particularly as Mr. Willard had decided to put them up a log house in which they might be independent of the people and more secure in case of trouble. But here came our boat problem again. With so much to be done all over our field, we were tied hand and foot for weeks. When passage was found for our teachers, the small amount of lumber we had to put into the house was still obliged to wait and has done so till today when a volunteer canoe has come from the upper village to take it. Tomorrow my husband expects to go up with it and get the building under way.

The people have treated the new teachers very kindly, furnishing them, free of charge, all the fish they could use and giving them two barrels in which to pack salted fish for winter use, besides many other favors. The people say they will not allow the teachers to starve as the minister has to do down here.

A good school has been started with from sixty to seventy scholars even in this busy time. Mr. Willard expects to visit it and preach once a month. He would have done so even if he had had to climb the trackless mountains, I believe, had it not been for our long illnesses.

We have had word from our secretary, Mrs. F.E.H. Haines, that a lady teacher will be sent us sometime during this summer. We are so happy in anticipation! But how she is to reach here we cannot tell. We pray God to take care of her and bring her safely through all the perils of the way.

Now I must speak of that dear project of mine mentioned in a former letter—a Home for our Chilkat children. I wish I could tell you that it is begun or that we had even five dollars in hand to pay for twenty logs. If it were so, we should order them tonight, for many of the men are now free for awhile. We dare not go on without the money to pay for each day's work as soon as it is done. The Indians want it in silver, which is almost impossible to obtain here. It could be sent us, however, by mail from our friends, in registered packages sewed up in bags covered with paper.

Some time ago we received a letter which gave us some of the most thankful joy we ever knew. It told us that the ladies of your church had devoted a gift to the Home. We had thought of starting the boys' department first, because that could be soonest made self-supporting. But with that welcome letter from you came another also, from a personal friend long unheard from, who proposed to support a girl in our Home, laboring under the impression that we were in charge of one similar to that at Fort Wrangell. The money had already been forwarded to the Board for one year's support. Another letter came from another state to the same effect and also informing us that the McFarland Home was too full to admit any more children.

This seemed to us plain providence. Forty dollars toward the Home and the support of the two girls already paid into the treasury. We could not do as well for the boys this year. A larger guarantee would be necessary for a beginning there.

It was not quite so plain how we should take care of the children until the plan would develop enough to enable us to employ a matron, but we determined to get logs and what shingles we could with the Springfield money. If no more came, we could take out some of our own windows for this year and build a good log house of four rooms, which in the future would be but a wing of the great Home.

This decided upon, I sat down and wrote the whole plan to Mrs. Haines, asking if she could send us a teacher with sufficient consecration and physical strength to take charge of the few girls whose support should be secured for this year. So we are waiting and praying.

Of all things, I should love to take the care of these children myself, but I have already the work of three persons, with only the strength of one wee bit of a woman. But we hope to be all one in the good work, working together for good. If we could only begin! It is so important it should be soon, not only that all may be in readiness before the setting in of our early winter, but because time means salvation to these girls. One of our most earnest girls has been shut up these three months. If we could promise to provide for her, I do not know but that her parents would give her up to us, though their custom requires her to be kept in dark solitude for two years.

The interior country promises much in gold. The excitement on the coast and in all the mining region of the territory is, we are told, becoming intense. There is prophesied a great rush soon, with our mission station as the center. A party of ten miners from Arizona passed by a week ago. They make nineteen who are connected. The others have been in the interior a year. We hear that a company is coming up from Juneau and that a boat is being fitted out at San Francisco and going around to meet these nineteen on the headwaters of the Yukon. That river is navigable from its mouth to within seventy-five miles of us.

Oh, that we had seen the Home started first!

Carrie M. Willard

SHELDON JACSON INSTITUTE
SITKA, ALASKA
AUGUST 14, 1882

MY DEAR PARENTS: Of course you wonder how and why we are in Sitka. It would be impossible for you to realize why, for you could not understand what our necessities and our sufferings have been. I am so glad that you cannot! There seemed to be no help on the earth, and though we cried, the heavens seemed brass.

When I thought our little Carrie might be left alone, I wrote a note to Mrs. Austin asking her to keep our baby if need be, until she could be taken to you. Mrs. Austin's great loving mother's heart was roused at once so that sleeplessly and prayerfully she sought how she might help us. At last, with Mr. Brady, they succeeded in getting the *Rose*, which belongs to Mr. Brady's partners, to run up to Chilkat to carry our freight and bring us down to Sitka. We paid the bare running expenses of the vessel—one hundred twenty-five dollars. Mr. Brady and Mrs. Austin came and managed everything—put our goods in, packed our trunks and made it possible for us to come. As it was, even with the greatest care and providentially fine weather, it seemed as though we should hardly reach Sitka alive. But here we are, and such nursing, such food, and such care we could know nowhere else save with you. We were all greatly reduced both from suffering and want of food.

Dear little Carrie gets all the milk she wants now, and already her cheeks are growing round and rosy. For myself, I am distressed only at what they oblige me to eat of the meat for which I was dying, and the beautiful fresh berries which are so delicious! I am sure I shall soon regain all that I had lost and be as strong as ever and ready for any duty that may be given to me.

Mr. Brady knew nothing about the barrel of clothing waiting here and, although it had been in the warehouse since May, it was the only thing of all our goods which was not brought up on the *Rose*. The barrel was just what we wanted. It was opened the day after we came and almost overwhelmed us with gladness. You will never know how precious and timely your goodness was! I wish I had the strength to write to each one who helped to give us so much comfort and happiness. We think the whole contents of the barrel perfect, but I must wait to write more about it.

We do not know when we will get back to Chilkat—before too long, we hope. Mother Austin says it is impossible for Baby and me to go this winter in the open boat, and that is the only way now to be seen. But all things will be provided.

Carrie M. Willard

SHELDON JACKSON INSTITUTE
SITKA, ALASKA
OCTOBER 3, 1882

DEAR PARENTS: The *Wachusette* will sail for San Francisco today, having been relieved by the man-of-war *Adams*. The captain of the latter, as also of the former, is favorable to missions and declares himself a friend to the missionaries.

We are in doubt as to just how we are to return to our field. The *Rose* has met an accident, having run on a rock, and the owners are in doubt as to whether they will fix her up again.

Our baby Fred will be three weeks old tomorrow. He weighed nine pounds. Carrie is almost wild with joy over her "baby b'lov-a H'litz." She kisses us goodnight and goes away to sleep in another room by herself, happy in seeing new Baby safe with me. She is distressed sometimes lest somebody take him away. We are to have communion before Dr. Sheldon Jackson goes back, when he is to baptize little Fred.

Oh, my mother, I have wanted you! But the Lord has been with us, and these dear friends have shown us all loving kindness.

What we would do without Miss Bessie Matthews now here, I do not know. Dear Mrs. Austin has congestion of the retina and is in danger of going blind. Oh, what she has done for me and mine! It can never be repaid in this world.

OCTOBER 14

In regard to the publishing of the letters: I am persuaded to permit it. They are so imperfect— were often written with a baby on my lap and more often with the Indians all about me asking all sorts of questions—that I would prefer to take bits from the letters, adding more and better. But they are wanted soon, and there will not be time.

Carrie M. Willard

SHELDON JACKSON INSTITUTE
SITKA, ALASKA
OCTOBER 24, 1882

MY DEAR PARENTS: Resting on one elbow, I am trying to write a little to send by the *U.S.S. Corwin* on its way south from the polar sea. I am sitting up part of the time now.

It does seem as though God had sent our troubles to make our cup larger and then ordered it refilled with joy. "Not our duty to go back again to that dreadful country," you say? No, not until God

121

opens the way to go. I try to comfort myself and gain patience and strength for biding His time with the thought that He best knows what His work needs. When He sees us prepared and our work necessary, He will send a boat to take us home. And, oh, how gladly we will go!

OCTOBER 30

There is great trouble in Kill-is-noo, about halfway between here and Chilkat where the North-West Trading Company has its chief post, store, and whale-fishery and oil works. While the company was putting up the wharf in the spring, one of the Indians was accidentally killed by the falling of a tree. As he was in the company's employ, in the eyes of Indian law, the company was responsible. A payment of two hundred blankets was demanded. The company agreed to pay forty, but Captain Merriman of the man-of-war *Adams* ordered that no payment should be made.

Things have gone on until Sabbath before last, when the launch and whale boat were out after a whale. A harpoon bomb burst, and one of the Indians—a medicine man—was killed. In a short time about three hundred of the tribe had surrounded the boats, which were then captured and the white men taken prisoners.

The captain of the launch sent a line of advice to Captain Vanderbilt that they would take the *Favorite* too. The note was carried by one of the Indians who had been in the boat with the medicine man and escaped to the woods. Captain Vanderbilt at once conveyed his own family to the *Favorite* and, leaving in the night, ran down here for the man-of-war. Arriving next evening, he left his family and started back at twelve o'clock the same night, accompanied by the *Corwin*, in charge of Captain Merriman. Four hundred blankets were demanded for taking the whites prisoners. The Indians said they would not pay. The captain gave the Indians two hours to remove their things from their homes, then commanded the guns to fire. Away went the village—all but four houses. Forty canoes were also broken. The captain said if he were "called there to settle any more such troubles there would not be a man left to tell there ever was such a tribe." The effect of this on our people will be of the utmost moment to us, but God will care for his own work.

Dr. Sheldon Jackson was here four weeks. He and others got the Home building almost under roof. It is a solid building, one hundred by fifty feet, in a beautiful location. The Sabbath before he left we had our first communion here, and he baptized our precious baby "Frederick Eugene Austin Willard." It seemed to me that I had hardly known the meaning of communion before. Here in the uttermost end of the earth in a little upper room, a handful of believers had fellowship with God and with his children throughout the world.

Carrie M. Willard

SHELDON JACKSON INSTITUTE
SITKA, ALASKA
NOVEMBER 17, 1882

TO THE SABBATH SCHOOL OF THE PRESBYTER-
IAN CHURCH OF EAST SPRINGFIELD, NEW YORK, MY
DEAR FRIENDS: I think you must have heard

already of our long continued trials in sickness as well as of our joy over a beautiful new baby whom we call Fred. He came to us on the thirteenth day of September, just the day after that precious barrel came from you—the barrel about which I was too ill to know anything for six weeks. Then we had a grand opening day, and we wished, as you did, that you could have been partakers with us of that feast. There were some tears shed, but not for grief.

I was still unable to sit up and, as her papa unpacked the barrel in my room, our two-year-old Carrie trotted back and forth bringing me the things to look at. She stood on tiptoe trying to peer into the treasure house, and as one by one of the articles were lifted to her sight, she clapped her hands before seizing the items, then ran with them to me, her face aglow and all the way calling, "Mama! Oh, oh, Mama! See! Oh!" Her papa's and mama's pleasure was just as sincere as hers.

All the way from Grace Robinson's blocks and Joel Rathbun's baby mittens to dear old grandmother's green flannel, from the advertising cards to that unabridged Webster, everything was full of beauty to us, so rich had they been made by your love. We thank you a thousand times.

That glad opening day, so full of joy to our Carrie, was, I believe, the last day she was able to be up. During my long illness there had been no physician here, but while little Carrie was ill, there were three, or we think our precious child could not have lived through her terrible attack. For days we watched and nursed her. But God spared her, and she is now slowly recovering, though still weak as a babe and thin and pale. Of course I am worn with suffering and long watching, so please pardon if I write but a dull letter.

Our Home is not begun, and our hearts are full of sadness to think of our people so long without us. We are so happy and grateful for the deep and unexpected interest that our Home project has created and for the generous responses to our call for means. We have been informed of the receipt by the Woman's Executive Committee of Home Missions of nearly one thousand dollars for this purpose, and you know that we have the promise of more. Since this is the case, and we have been prevented from beginning a Home, we are hoping to hear of further contributions— enough to justify our beginning in the early sping with a building to cost not above four thousand dollars. To be able to accomplish this next summer we must know that every cent is certain, in time to send below to Oregon and have the lumber come up on the spring steamer. Our building, as we have planned it, will be forty by sixty feet, for both boys and girls, and will cost so much because freights are about double those to Sitka. The money sent to the Board should be plainly labeled "For the building of the Chilkat Home."

In September, Dr. Sheldon Jackson came up on the steamer to superintend the building of the new Sitka Home, bringing with him Miss Bessie L. Matthews of Monmouth, Illinois, to take charge of our school in Haines. When our Home is in full running order, we will have another teacher, and Miss Matthews will be its worthy matron, so you must know and love her henceforth as a member of your missionary family. Now she awaits our return, when she will accompany us and begin school work. What we all should have done without her I do not know, as good Mrs. Austin has had sickness in her own family, and her eyes have been so badly affected that the physician forbade her doing anything.

Dr. Jackson also brought Miss Kate A. Rankin as an assistant matron to Mrs. A. R. McFarland at Fort Wrangell, and Miss Clara A. Gould to take charge of the school at Jackson, under her brother, who recently entered that field. He and Mr. McFarland (who married Miss Dunbar at Wrangell) were laymen ordained for this work.

We have now five Presbyterian ministers in Alaska—Mr. John G. Brady came out to the Sitka mission in 1878, but is now engaged in mercantile business here. Mr. S. Hall Young has charge of the Wrangell work. Then there are my husband and the two newcomers first mentioned. This number enables us to have a Presbytery, and at our first meeting we hope to have Mr. Austin, of this station, ordained. Although he was commissioned by the Board as a lay-teacher, he has been doing most excellently a minister's work here. Our meeting is to convene at Sitka, as it is the most central station, being about two hundred seventy-five miles south of Haines, one hundred fifty miles northwest of Fort Wrangell, and about two hundred seventy-five miles north of Jackson. Hoonah, where Mr. Styles, a son-in-law of Mr. Austin, taught last year, is north of Sitka about halfway to Haines. From Juneau, Haines is by steamer one hundred and five miles, but by canoe only seventy-five miles. We have had no word from our field since August. From that time, Mrs. Dickinson, our interpreter, had two months' vacation in Oregon.

Our Sunday services are conducted through an interpreter, but our teaching is not. We are learning Tlingit as fast as we can and hope to be able to do without an interpreter soon. Had it not been for our sickness, we would now be able to do so. As it is, we communicate with the people ordinarily without trouble. Of course, in the school we teach English, and the little folks pick it up rapidly, though they are diffident about trying to use it because they are keenly sensitive to ridicule. The slightest smile at a mistake will bring on such sulks as utterly to preclude the possibility of another sound from that child. When I gain more strength, I must tell you more about our people.

Before another quarter we hope the Master will send us back to our own work in Chilkat, but by what means we do not know.

Carrie M. Willard

SHELDON JACKSON INSTITUTE
SITKA, ALASKA
NOVEMBER 22, 1882

DEAR PARENTS: I sent you word by the last mail of our little Carrie's illness because we had no reason to hope that we should not have the sadder news to tell you this time, and I thought it would be such a shock. For several days the doctor gave us no hope, but God has been merciful. She is slowly getting well. She is not yet able to walk, but is living.

127

I had only begun to sit up for a few minutes at a time when she was taken so suddenly and dangerously ill. The doctor who had most providentially been sent here just a few days before was very attentive. Two others were here temporarily on the government vessels, and with them he consulted several times. It seemed she would surely have died without their aid.

As to our going back to Chilkat: We feel certain that our work is there. Has not God kept us through everything? It is not at all probable that we shall ever again be exposed to the trials and sufferings which we have endured. We will be happy to go back when God opens the way for us.

The hardest thing is in regard to food for the children. Of course, there we have no fresh meat, eggs or milk. Baby Fred is doing well on cow's milk. I do not like the thought of taking it from him, but he is such a strong, healthy fellow he will not miss it as much as will his sister. We have sent for imperial granum and Ridge's baby food, and Mr. Willard will try to have venison sent from Juneau through the winter.

Haines is being made a post office, through the efforts of Dr. Sheldon Jackson. Mr. Willard is to be postmaster. So we shall likely have a mail every month, and after we get our steam launch things will be different. We do appreciate your efforts to gain that for us and thank you so much!

Another of God's great mercies to us was His sending dear Bessie Matthews just when He did. She has been everything in this household.

Mrs. Austin has almost lost the use of her eyes. For more than a month the doctor has not

allowed her to do anything, and Miss Matthews
has been both hands and eyes to her, besides
sharing in the nursing. Of all the unselfish people
I have known, my mother, Mrs. Austin and
Bessie Matthews stand at the head of the list.

Did I tell you that when dear Mother Austin
heard of our sickness she was determined to come
to us in a canoe?—a distance of over two hundred
miles along a route over which many and many a
canoe has been lost. Since we have been here, her
devotion and love have never dimmed day or
night. No money could ever repay her, and I
greatly long to be able to do something for her.

Our Chilkat Home is surely to be built...

Carrie M. Willard

SHELDON JACKSON INSTITUTE
SITKA, ALASKA
NOVEMBER 29, 1882

TO THE LADIES' HOME MISSION SOCIETY,
SCHENECTADY, NEW YORK, MY DEAR MRS. POTTER:
If ever I write you, you say. If ever I do *not* write
after receiving such tokens of loving thought as
those two packages from Schenectady proved to
be, I shall not be myself. At any rate, I am so glad
of that writing paper which you kindly sent! We
thank you and through you wish to thank all the
good people who had part in the good deed. It is
only in circumstances like ours, cut off from home
comforts, that Christian friendship can be appreciated at its full worth. Even the slightest tokens,
when sent so far and received by us in our isola-
tion and loneliness, bring with them a power to
warm and thrill our hearts.

Willard

Would you like to hear how the bundles were opened? Well, it was in Sitka instead of Chilkat, because we have had no means of getting home since our beautiful baby boy came in September.

On the day after the steamer left, when Mr. Austin opened his box and brought to us our share of its contents, baby Fred lay asleep in his cradle. Sick Carrie sat propped among her pillows with her mama close beside, while on the floor papa disclosed the treasures. The first thing which attracted my attention was the blue and white coverlet. It looked so familiar and home-like, for my own dear mother spun the yarn for and wove just such a one long before she was my mother. I know its labor cost enough to appreciate its worth, and it will be additionally valuable to us. Next came the nice white bedspread and sheets and pillowcases, the towels, the warm woolly blankets, etc., all of which, as they came to view, brought new exclamations of delight.

Last of all we looked at the things for young Carrie, and I do wish that you all could have seen her as she received them. Her pleasure was an ecstasy. She must have them on right away. When I put on her the little blue dress, it would have added much to our pleasure if the good mother whose darling had first worn it could have seen mine wear it then. She is called a beautiful child, and I think she is, with her long sunny curls, big blue eyes and wonderful skin. She looked so sweet in that perfectly fitting dress! All the clothes were exactly the right size. Katch-keel-ah, our little Indian girl, was also thoroughly pleased with her mittens. Let us thank you again.

We do not know how soon the way will be opened for our return to Haines, but we hope soon. We long to be back with our own people.

Have you heard that we are to have a Home for children at Haines? It is to be built next summer, and we will need everything for it, from soap to curtains to carpet, from shoes to bonnets to capes. We are to have both boys and girls. When time and strength will permit, I shall be glad to tell you more of our plans and of our work. But for this time I must close.

Gratefully and affectionately yours,
Carrie M. Willard

SHELDON JACKSON INSTITUTE
SITKA, ALASKA
DECEMBER 21, 1882

MY DEAR FRIENDS: Today I shall try to fulfill my promise of writing you something further regarding our Chilkat people. And first it shall be respecting their belief as to death and the future life and their mode of disposing of the dead.

With them, as with us, man is an immortal soul, living forever in bliss or distress. Their heaven they call "the beautiful, beautiful island," which is surrounded by a green water so vast and limitless that no spirit can find its way to rest and happiness. Even to the outer edge—to the earth side—of this eternity it is a long, weary way, for the comfort and successful issue of which great preparations are made. The living heap gifts upon the dead. As soon as it becomes evident that someone is about to die, every energy is bent toward ensuring a comfortable journey.

Willard

Last winter, when a child was sick and suffering, I insisted on his parents bringing out blankets and keeping him warm. But they had none. So after keeping him in my own house and tending him till he grew better, I dressed him in warm clothing. Then I told the mother that she must keep him so dressed, that his life depended on it, and she took him home.

At midnight there was a knock on our window and, springing up, I found the father of the child in great distress, begging me to come, as they thought the child was dying. In a few moments I was with the little one, who lay in his mother's arms unconscious and scarcely breathing. It was evidently congestion of the lungs, from which he had no strength to rally.

When I saw him next, it was in full equipment for the journey. The small face was painted with vermilion, the head turbaned with a bright handkerchief. Every article of good clothing he possessed, together with what I had given him, was on him now. They had also made mittens and tied them on his hands. In a little bag hung about his neck were charms for his safety and a paper containing a quantity of red powder for use on the way. The body had been placed in a sitting posture with the knees drawn up against the breast and held in place by a cloth bandage. Then over and around all were beautiful, woven white woolen blankets, enough to make any mother's heart comfortable.

The body always sits thus in state until all the arrangements are perfected for its burning, always at sunrise. On the night before, the friends of the tribe are called together at the house of the deceased and the roll of rank is called.

The highest chief is called first. One man takes his position close to the great blazing fire in the center of the room. The logs are piled together for this social fire in log house fashion, four-square and three or four high. The flames sometimes reach even through the hole in the roof.

Beside him, the chief has a wooden tray of tobacco from which he fills the pipe bowls of the friends. One by one, as they are filled, a boy lights and starts them, then hands them to the waiting circle. The pipes are smoked and exchanged again and again in silence, except for the occasional slow and solemn speech of some member, which elicits now and then a monotonous refrain from another, all retaining their seats. Then the chiefs with wooden staves beat time on the floor while the other men sing a wild strain into which the women, with their blackened faces and close-cut hair, burst with shrill cries, which fall again into a low dying wail.

At sunrise the body, which has been wrapped and wrapped again in the best blankets, is raised by ropes made of skin through the opening in the roof, as superstition forbids carrying a dead body through the door. The cremation takes place at some distance from the houses. What stands for their burying ground is usually of a rolling character—that is, on a small hill—and presents an appearance like a village of miniature houses, each built on four high stakes. These houses are the receptacles of the box into which have been put the bones and ashes of the burned body. The

Grave Houses at Klukwan
(from A. Krause, *Die Tlingit Indianer*)

houses are never opened save by the "witches," who leave no traces of their visits, and by the friends of some "bewitched" person, who search for the misplaced bone that caused some trouble.

The night after the cremation, a *co-ek-y*—feast for the dead—is celebrated. Another tribe is invited. Red paint is used with the black. There is music and dancing. Great quantities of berries and salmon oil are brought out in huge dishes and placed on the floor among the guests, every bowl is surrounded. Then as the people eat together, wooden dishes of similar food, and of flour, sugar, and whatever else they have been able to obtain, are placed in the fire and burned.

They believe that thus spiritualized, these foods may be partaken of by the spirit of their friend so lately freed from the body by fire and still hovering about before starting on the journey.

Medicine Man Grave Houses

After this the music and dancing are resumed and then comes the display for which the entire family has been saving and gathering, perhaps for many years, and for which they may suffer in want for years to come. Great heaps of blankets, webs of cloth, muslin and calico, are brought out and laid before a man appointed to dispose of them. With two assistants he cuts and tears all these items into small strips. He does so with a peculiar carved and inlaid hook kept for that purpose. The strips are distributed among the people, who treasure them as precious possessions, and by sewing them together will construct a garment after the style of Joseph's coat of many colors. Sometimes we see a coat made of three pieces obtained at different times. The body of the coat will be striped red, yellow, purple and green, with one sleeve of blue and the other of brown. Dresses

135

Totem Dish with Table Mat

are made up in the same unique fashion—of perhaps a dozen different patterns and colors.

This feast ends the ceremonies, which according to the Chilkat's belief, are participated in by the dead. Afterward, if the deceased was a male of high class, the heir or heiress must, with feasting and dancing, build a dwelling house to stand as a monument to the departed.

To this prevailing custom there are no exceptions, except in the preserving of the bodies of the medicine men and in cases of drowning when the body cannot be recovered. The bodies of medicine men are never burned, because their spirits leave the bodies to enter new ones. It is thus that the *Kah-nauk-salute* (medicine man) is born. If, after the death of an Indian doctor, a woman dreams that his spirit has entered her unborn child, or if a child is born with red or curly hair, the child is sacred from birth on, and his hair is inviolate from shears or comb. After his death the body is held in awe and is wrapped in the best of everything. His face is painted red, and his hair powdered with eagles' down, which he used to a great

Woven Chilkat Shawl of Mountain Goat Wool

extent in his incantations. At last, he is bound in his wraps like a mummy and laid away in some rocky gorge or in a cave worn by waves.

There is always great virtue pertaining to the body of a medicine man, and its presence is indispensable at the initiation of new doctors. I have been with the Indians in passing by one of these sepulchres, and it is always with hushed tones and gestures of awe and terror that they speak of what it holds. If they have with them young children as they pass the haunted spot, a handful of down is held over the child and blown away to carry off any evil influence that may be cast upon the child by the dark spirits that guard the place.

More than any other form of death, more than excruciating torture, the Indians dread drowning. Going through the water, the dying one is never utterly freed from the clogs of earth. He is not equipped for the journey through a mystery land.

For ages he must wander hungry and cold with scarcely a possibility of at last finding the great green water which lies between every soul and heaven. When a soul has gained for itself the right to eternal happiness, it sees, upon approaching the great river, a canoe in waiting to convey the soul to the happy land. A sure entrance and an everlasting security are assured. The wicked also gain the shore but are doomed to eternal waiting.

Carrie M. Willard

SHELDON JACKSON INSTITUTE
SITKA, ALASKA
MARCH 12, 1883

MY DEAR FRIENDS: Why, yes indeed, I will tell you about Sitka! Did you think it was on Sitka Island? I thought so once, before Mr. Willard, little Carrie and I came to Alaska.

I do hope that I shall not puzzle you further. Sitka is situated on a beautiful harbor bearing the same name and indenting the western coast of Baranof Island. Great mountains to the east and north stand guard over the town nestling at their feet and shelter it from the cold winds and snow that, blowing from the far icy inland, strike these old protectors and turn their stern heads white. Seaward too, island fortifications thrown up long ago shield this favored child-city from the roughness of the waters.

It is not cold here. At the foot of the mountains there is, indeed, enough ice on the lake (whose waters, flowing down, keep turning the great wheel of the town's sawmill) to make skating—for some days at least—during the short

Sitka Harbor and Islands Beyond, 1883

winter. Enough snow falls to make a handsled quite a pleasure on the long, smooth street. The small folks—ay, and the big ones too—enjoy it greatly. The Indian children ride just like white boys, only...do you know...I've never seen them going "grinders." They do slide in every other way and on every conceivable kind of sled. Boxes and bits of board and shingles are the most fashionable.

Alonzo Austin has quite a novel turnout for this part of Alaska: a seated sleigh drawn by a big black dog nicely trained to the whip. This dog will run for a mile or two without seeming to grow tired. Not only that, but he really seems to enjoy the fun as much as anybody. Everyone has to be quick about enjoying the sledding, for the snow doesn't stay long. The ground may change in an hour from its native gray to the snowy white made gay with noisy children, and then an hour later, all the snow may have vanished as rain pours down.

There is a great deal of rain here. You know that in the States a foot and a half is about an average annual rainfall, but the rainfall of Sitka for the year 1882 was about eight and a half feet. Yet the humidity is much less than that of many portions of the United States where there is much less rain. If the Sitkans were more careful about drainage, Sitka should be a healthful place.

The town itself is a little old tumbledown affair more remarkable for its mossy Russian ruins than for anything else. And yet there is one feature made more strikingly prominent by these very things—that root which, springing up, shall one day bear the white flower of immortal life, the fruit of glory to God. We saw the blade in the first mission school started here and which developed into the first Home for boys. The building, which was a part of crumbling Russia, was destroyed by fire in January of 1882. And now we see not only a fresh green blade of promise, but the "ear"—in the great new building for a hundred boys and girls which Dr. Sheldon Jackson erected last summer. You and those whom your means have sent here work together towards filling the "full corn in the ear." Let us labor faithfully and with prayer that at the last there may be a great and joyous gathering in and rendering up of the precious grain.

The new mission building is at the extreme edge of town, with Popoff Mountain behind, almost overhanging the town. At the other end of town, in

Sitka, 1880
(from *Alaska* by Sheldon Jackson)

a part which during Russian rule was barricaded, is the Native's village. Its front is open to the bay and there is a higher ridge of ground close behind which is thickly built with grave houses.

As a natural barrier, great rocks push out from the ridge toward the bay, just at the entrance to the village. There, where rock and water fail to meet, is the barricade with but a single opening into the smooth green common. The common is now used by the young people for outdoor games and by the marines for a parade ground. It seems, however, to have been in the old days a park, whose picturesque music stand still remains. But the trees, together with the cottages occupied by the Russian officers that lined two sides of the park, were burned down long ago.

141

A stone wall on the third side, set with cannon, kept the law between land and sea. Along the fourth side, just opposite the barricade, still stand the custom house and the barracks. Between them, guarded by mounted brass cannon, is the double gate entrance to the Russian "castle." Built on a high rock overlooking both town and harbor, it was reached by means of wearisome flights of stairs. This immense old log structure, with the arched windows of its high-gabled center roof looking out to sea, is the third building which has occupied this rock's top. Of the others, the first was destroyed by fire and the second, a brick building, by earthquake. But all three have been the residence of the ruling prince. The hewn logs of this building are fitted into each other like round-bottomed troughs, with moss and clay between, and are dovetailed at the corners, through each of which passes a great copper bolt from roof to foundation.

During Russian reign Sitka was full of life and gaity, having, besides its prince's family, his suite, government officials with their families, and the military. There were also the officers of the Greek Church, for many of its priests and bishops are members of the Russian army. The church at that time was rich, magnificent with its pictures, its gold wrought and jeweled frames and hangings. Much of this wealth was stolen, it is said, by the soldiers after the territory was purchased by the United States Government. There were, too, at that early time, good schools and a seminary. There were also shipping yards with "ways" for launching vessels of a thousand tons.

Sitka's Main Street, 1883

After the transfer of title and the consequent removal of nearly all the Russians, civilization sank to rudeness. Schools ceased, industries failed. The principal aim of the United States military force stationed here seems to have been the total destruction of good. The worst part of a civilized world they did bring, such as whiskey.

In front of the government buildings, passing through the common, is the hard smooth avenue running through the town from the wharf back of the barracks to Sheldon Jackson Institute, and for a mile beyond through the evergreens, which, opening here and there, give lovely glimpses of the bay. There are no horses and carriages to travel this road now. In Russian days, I am told, they were both numerous and fine. The nearest approach here at present to such equipage is a big wagon drawn by a team of mules brought up for work in the mines. There are, besides, three or four cows, several goats, two sheep, and innumerable dogs. The stock of vehicles includes a hand cart, a water barrel on wheels, a baby carriage or two and some wheelbarrows.

The new Institute house, though large, is but a nucleus for the several hoped-for buildings to be grouped about it as the means open and increase. It is designed so this may become the principal trade school of Alaska. Sitka, as you know, occupies the central position, geographically, among the Presbyterian missions of Alaska. Although a Home—a good Home—at each of the stations seems a necessity to enable progress of the work, yet it would seem to be a wise economy to concentrate force so as to provide the best facilities for the teaching of trades in the one centrally located school to which all may have access as the peculiar tastes and aptitudes of the children are discovered in each mission by its own teachers...

Carrie M. Willard

Sheldon Jackson Institute, 1883

CHILKAT MISSION,
HAINES, ALASKA
MAY 8, 1883

TO THE SABBATH SCHOOL OF THE PRESBYTER-
IAN CHURCH OF EAST SPRINGFIELD, NEW YORK, MY
DEAR FRIENDS: Can you imagine the joy of being
able at last to write at *home*? You can hardly
appreciate it, and our every moment is too full to
try to tell you how great that joy.

We reached Haines on Sabbath, April 8, after
a voyage of about four days, having taken the
steamer on the 4th. We had had about two weeks
of perfect weather: the air balmy, the sun bright
and the sea a glassy calm. How we longed to be

145

on the way! At length, on March 31 (Saturday), the *Rose* made her trial trip, during which it was discovered that her new condensing pipes were altogether insufficient, and so, for the third time, it was necessary to beach her. Monday morning found her again on the sands, where the old machinery was replaced. On Tuesday we were rejoiced at receiving word that our freight would be taken on next day. Tuesday night came with heavy rain, which continued with raw, chilling winds throughout the three days following. In spite of the best care which I could give them, both little ones took heavy colds during the packing. Everything got wet going down to the boat. We ourselves tramped down through the rain with two sleepy babies and bundles innumerable that Wednesday night at ten o'clock. That was the hour of high tide, the only time that we could get down from the dock to the boat. The only stateroom on the *Rose* opens out upon deck and is open as to weather, but close as to air. It measures six by eight feet, with three bunks on each side, the only window a skylight of two panes.

On the voyage down I had preferred the open deck at night, when the waves and rain both wet us, but this time, by dint of good management in stepping out to turn around and by waiting without until some of the party were stowed away in their bunks, we all six succeeded in finding shelter. We had to furnish our own pillows and bed clothing, which after the trip to the boat were damp enough to begin with; but the rain came through both roof and sides. We could not leave the wharf till low tide, at 4:20 a.m., because that would bring us into the rapids at next high tide—the only time possible for us to get through them out into the open channel. At last, 4:20 came. We left Sitka in the gray light Thursday morning and reached the rapids at eleven o'clock, when we found that we had missed going through with the tide by just twenty minutes. We steamed away for an hour, but barely holding our own, making no headway at all. There was nothing for it but to throw out our anchor and await the next rise, at three p.m., which we did. A little after that hour we rushed into Peril Strait, where we found rough water and had all we could do to reach Lindenburg Harbor. Even then we were so tossed about that I lost my balance and fell into real sea-sickness. The rain still came down, and our beds were wet; but the night passed. The storm continued until the afternoon, when the clouds lifted and the wind fell. Taking up anchor at four o'clock, we ran boldly out to the channel. After a mile or so, it was found that a pin was loose in the engine, and we stopped to fix it. This proved to be only a trifling hindrance; but when we looked about again, the fog had gathered so thick as to drive us back to our shelter in the harbor, where we lay at anchor until three o'clock on Saturday morning.

In the afternoon the men took the small boats and went ashore for water, wood and clams. Mr. Willard took Miss Matthews and our Indian girl to secure specimens of the lovely moss and shells which we could see from deck. The clam beach was perfect, and the island woods and moss were—well, like the woods and moss of Alaska—

deep, dense and grand. The different kind of starfish and sea urchins looked like flowers. The real flowers were full of fragrance that spoke sweetly of springs long gone in the dear old homeland. So another night settled down upon us—the very night which we had so hoped would bring us home. But God had been guiding us...and hindering us, for had we been twenty minutes earlier and made the tide at the rapids, we should have been hurled into Peril Straits with a storm and perhaps never have reached a harbor. Then, afterward, had we not been detained near a place of safety until the fog bank arose, we would have been surrounded by great danger.

The rain had ceased, the sea was quiet, and we but waited to have our way made plain before us. Here and there a star twinkled through in the zenith, but around and about us the grayish white wall was impenetrable until near morning. We took up anchor at three a.m. on Saturday. The sun arose a little uncertainly, but by noon had declared himself master of the day, and we were able to open the door of our ark and venture out on deck. After all, we said, we had had more of comfort than we had on the fine steamer *Dakota* from San Francisco two years ago. Besides we like the *Rose*, with its free meals anytime you may be able to eat, and its cozy kitchen fire, where babies can be warmed and fed without insulting the cook.

Lindenburg Harbor is but a few miles from Chatham Straits; so we were soon in that broad channel, whose waters only a few hours before must have been in a fury, but now were so placid

Mountain Scenery in Chilkat Country

and smooth as to give back reflections like a looking glass. Cross Sound and Hoonah Mountains,
in the distance, were enchanting. Billowy clouds
and snowy peaks touched with the pink and gold
of strengthening sunlight were easily transfig-
ured into castles with battlements and towers,
while the soft green of sky and water brought
them out in charming relief.

The day passed in beauty and in swift, quiet
sailing. Just as the sun was setting in such glory
as is never seen elsewhere, it seems to me, we
entered Lynn Canal. Passing Cross Sound on the
left hand and Point Retreat on the right (which
are respectively the open gateway of Hoonah and
the signpost of Juneau's mines), we were within
the close, grand passage which, almost without a
break in its mountain wall, leads to our front
door on Portage Bay. I cannot tell you what a feeling took possession of us as, leaving all the world
behind, we entered this great hallway of our own
dear Chilkat country. Oh, the joy of getting back
to it! All the suffering we ever endured in it was
as nothing compared to that of being kept out of
it so long, away from our people and our work.
May God as richly bless the people at our return
as we feel that he blesses us in bringing us back!

We sat on deck watching the ever varying
light and shade on passing scenes and singing
songs gay and sweet till the purpling of the shadows and the calling of gulls warned me that little
birdies should be in their nests. I tucked mine in
with grateful gladness at the thought that hith-
erto our Father had brought us, and that another
waking may be the opening of our eyes on home.

But it was not—quite. As the cold gray morning began to steal through our skylight, I became conscious of something peculiar in our situation. I could not tell whether it was sound or motion that startled me, until there was a bump and a recoil. A sudden ceasing of the engine's noise, a hasty raking out of its fire, and we were sinking—so gradually and almost imperceptibly that I scarcely realized our position until I found Baby rolling out of his berth. I called the others, and Mr. Willard went out to see what the trouble was. We were lying at about forty-five degrees, and walking was a feat. Carrie, fortunately, was on the low side with Miss Matthews. I, with Fred, was obliged to be boarded in and lie in the trough formed by bottom and side. Just around the lower point of Portage Bay the inlet is very wide. Just above are the glaciers, the Chilkoot, the Taiya and the K-hossy Heen Inlets, which, carrying sand from the mountains, have at this time made large deposits, forming sandfields of great extent, though all are covered at high tide. Still, close to the rocky western shore there is a channel which through all tides is wide and deep. Our pilot had missed it, and the tide, fast running out, left us lying on a hill four miles from home. Every object was familiar. We were at home, yet not in it.

We rolled around till afternoon, when high tide took us off, and we came safely into harbor just in time to see the people going from the schoolhouse, where Louis Paul (who had been down for a week from the upper village) had been having Sunday school. Of course the Indians crowded about on every hand, saying that "they had thought they should die before we came again." "They had looked for us without sleeping." "They needed us so much! They had had sickness and trouble, and they had no minister." We found the men nearly all gone into the Stick country (the interior) packing for the miners. Some were at the cannery building across the Chilkat River. They had taken up the little bodies that were buried a year ago and cremated them. They did not have nearly as much snow this winter. Still, they wanted us back.

By the following Sabbath we had cleaned the schoolhouse. We made new benches, washed the windows, put up short curtains of muslin and turkey red, hung the charts and pictures, tore out the old box pulpit and set in its place the good Estey organ sent us by the Little Leaven Band of Monmouth, Illinois, and had everything in order for Sabbath service and for school on Monday.

On Sabbath morning, long before time, the people were washed, dressed, and waiting for the bell. We had a full and eager house, for on the Friday night before, the men had returned. We saw on every hand the evidences of earnings well spent: new shawls and prints on wives and children, new cloth suits on some of the boys and men. Quite a number of upper village people had come down.

The "murderer" was there with a nice-fitting suit of black, new hat and boots, and a faultlessly white shirt front, with a standing collar, cravat and gold buttons. He looked quite a gentleman. He earlier had been bitterly opposed to having a teacher at the upper village. He wasn't afraid of the soldiers getting there to check his course. He boasted that he was but waiting to get us few whites together to kill us all at once, and that he would not have a teacher at Klukwan. When Louis and Tillie, the Native teachers, went there, he gave them much annoyance. At last he took the handbell from the boy who was ringing it through the village for school, declaring that they should have no more school. Sometime after, Louis went to have a talk with him. He thereafter returned the bell and became a regular attendant upon both day and Sunday schools.

Mr. Willard preached that day on the coming of the Lord, illustrating it by our own return. How had they kept the word we had given them? How should the Savior find them keeping his word?

In the afternoon we had the children's meeting. They recited, to the great delight of the old people, their alphabet, texts, the twenty-third psalm, the ten commandments, etc., in both languages, and fifty questions from the Catechism, and sang hymns in both English and Tlingit. Then we gave them the papers. Two hours had passed for the second time in service when the benediction was given; but they sat down again, and we sang another half hour. Still they said, "We have had no church for so long that we don't want you to send us away." Indeed, we were loath to do so.

Five or six little ones have died during our absence. Some people have gone away; others have come from other villages; and quite a number of babies have been born. Annie and Tillie, the sisters whose mother told me that she would

give them to the white men if I would not take
them, have indeed been taken to Juneau. Annie
was in seclusion before we left, and I trust that
she still might be.

This country is opening up rapidly. Aside from
gold interests, two canneries are being built on
Chilkat River for this season's salmon—one on the
other side and one on this, just across the trail.

Miss Matthews opened her school promptly
and is doing thorough work. Although this is a
busy season and the people are on the move continually, she has had sixty or seventy pupils, from
the baby of a month to the old chief, though we
didn't count the babies. The people are much
interested in the new teacher, but it was hard to
make them understand about her. I'm afraid they
thought that my husband had been following
their own provident plan in getting a second wife,
and they kept asking me over and over where her
minister was. Her sweet voice and ready accom-
paniments on the organ charm the people, and
she is fast winning a place among them.

But, of all the party, I think our Carrie is the
one most loved. From the first moment of our
landing, she has been the object of smiles and
pats and admiring remarks. She herself has scattered love and smiles most prodigally. It often
brings tears to my eyes to watch her among them.
At church, on Sabbath, it was both amusing and
sweet to see her moving about before service
began, patting a little one on the head, dropping
on her knees beside another, smiling up into its
face. I saw her wipe the nose of one child, and,
stopping in front of another, hold his hands while

he coughed, as she had seen me do with Baby
Fred when he had whooping cough. Then, taking
a singing book, opening it first and feigning to
read the lesson herself, she held it open to one
and another of the old people, reading aloud and
explaining, with many gestures and many nods of
her head, a few Tlingit words. But she took her
seat on the platform in time for service and
remained quiet throughout the whole of it, except
at singing. She always joins in that with all her
heart, knowing every hymn after hearing it once
or twice. She seems so little for it all! She loves
the big water and enjoyed the trip home very
much. The friends at Sitka had teased her about
keeping her baby brother with them. Of course,
she had protested earnestly, for she can scarcely
bear him out of her sight. Almost the first thing
after we went aboard, she looked about for Fred,
and not seeing him, so wrapped as he was in
blankets, she began to call loudly for him. Then
turning to me, she asked, "Baby *ooh* momma?"
That means, "Is he on the boat?" for she names
the boat after the sound of the whistle *ooh*. "Baby!
Dee, baby!" she called. Then, when I had shown
her where he lay asleep, she called each family
name to make sure of us all, and turning to Fritz
again, she said, with her funny nod and smile,
"Morning! Dee, baby! How do do?"

Baby too has come into an inheritance with
the Chilkat people. He is just seven months old. I
would not put short dresses on him until the
Indians had seen him in his white baby clothes,
so different from anything they ever saw before.
Some of the Chilkat wives are Sitka women, and

because this "beautiful snow-baby" was born in Sitka, they claim him for their own tribal brother. But the Chilkats hold on to him, saying that he is a Chilkat *quan* ("people"). Others say, "Good good baby, half Chilkat Tlingit, half Sitka Tlingit."

The Indians, small and big, crowd before every window. This position has one advantage over that of coming into the house; for when they come in, they do not always feel at liberty to follow us about from one room to another, but outside no such delicacy obtains. They see us leave one room for another, and, lo! they are at its window when we enter. When I place Baby where they can see him, they are perfectly delighted. Every movement of his chubby hands seems to surprise them. When he coos and laughs, they fairly scream with joy, while Kotzie [young Carrie] stands at the window gesticulating and talking Tlingit at a rapid rate. She never speaks a syllable of English to an Indian.

When we came home, we found an old crone sheltered by the Dickinsons and heard her story.

"I am old woman. I no good any more. I plenty sick, plenty tired. Minister come here. I go to church. I no hear his words in my heart, just like to me nonsense. I go outside and sit down in bushes. Spirits tell me, 'God no good; he not strong. Devil very strong. It better you work for him.' Spirits talk hard to me. I listen in bushes. Then I say, 'Yes, I work for devil.' I take dirty string off somebody's neck and a bit of salmon somebody spill out of mouth. I take rag off woman's dress and cut little hair off somebody's head. I steal away to medicine man's dead-house.

Devil strong then; he take me. I put on just one ragged skirt and piece of blanket on shoulders. Then I go inside. I hide all bits of string, fish, rag, hair in blanket. Now all these people going to die. Maybe in one year, maybe two, maybe five. By and by boy dies. I know I make him die. I very 'fraid. Next day everybody see all my wickedness. Then I know God strong; he show all people. I then say, 'Yes, I make boy die.' First I think God no strong. Then I find God very strong. I see no good to work for devil."

The straight road to their spirit world is over two high mountains and the intervening valley. When the shore of the great water is reached, the rocks are seen to be crowded with spirits waiting to be taken over to the beautiful island. Though far away, the island is plainly visible, as are its inhabitants, whose attention these waiting souls vainly try to gain by shouting. But wearied with watching, one no sooner begins to yawn than the sound of the yawn is heard on the island. A canoe is immediately sent to carry the sleeping spirit to its final home. It is circulated throughout the country that during the past winter a man who died in Sitka came back long enough to tell the people that they must burn more food and clothing and turn out more water on the fire when friends die. If they do so, they may have more comfort in the other world. He told them that all who adhered to the traditions of their fathers were the favored ones in the next life. They would sit close about the warm, bright fire, while those who follow the new Christ religion were slaves and sat back in the dark, cold corners.

I must tell you of Rebecca, the mother of Willis. Her first husband, who died when Willis was a baby, was a brother of Don-a-wok. She afterward married again and bore two daughters and a son, after which their father died. About that time she was out in the woods where men were felling trees. She had sat on a log, when the tree on which the men were at work crashed upon her, doubling her under it. They took her out and carried her home. They thought her back was broken. For several years she lay helpless, but one day she heard the story in her own hut of Jesus as the Healer, of his curing the sick or old. She said, "He is the same, isn't he? He says, too, 'Ask of me, and I will give you.'" She began to pray for recovery. From that day she began to gain strength, until she walked—not only about her house, but to church, a distance of four and a half miles.

Last winter a blind man wanted to marry her and tormented her for months. At last she spoke to me about it. She attended school and church and could not bear to give them up; and, besides, she disliked the man. She said he was rich, while her father was poor and had to support her and her children. And then the fellow said he would surely kill himself if she refused. I told her what a Christian marriage was and charged her to be brave, to do right—if she loved the man, to go; if not, to refuse him. She wished me to exact from him the promise, should he ever come to talk with me, that he would not keep her from going to church and school if she should marry him.

A short while after this, the man, with a crowd of relations, went to her father's house and rehearsed the whole matter: She was poor; he was rich. She was dependent, with her children, on her poor old father, who would soon die. Her suitor would make her independent. Yet she withstood this. Then he announced that if she did not marry him, he would go to the woods and die. Here his mother and sisters broke into hideous crying, entreating the woman to save their dear one. Still she would not consent. At last they said, "Well, he will kill himself. We will come on your old father for his life; he shall pay it." In desperation then, she said to the blind man, "Go to the minister. If the minister and his wife tell me to marry you, I will." Immediately, with one of his friends, he came to us and said that Rebecca wished our consent to her marrying him. As she had requested, I asked him if he would ever object to her going to school if she would consent. He promised that he would not and went back to the house with the word, supported by that of his friend, that we told her to marry him. He repeated that if she did not go with him at once he would go out and kill himself. She went, for her father's sake and that of her word. He took her away to his mother's house. He has never since allowed her to go to church or to school.

We find the season fully a month in advance of last year's spring. Though the mountains are still white, here in the lowlands flowers are springing on every hand, and the air is soft and full of fragrance. Birds are busy about us, and we take their sweet songs into our hearts.

With much love, your affectionate friend,

Carrie M. Willard

Willard

DEAR FRIENDS: The steamer now comes every month to the salmon canneries across the peninsula and leaves the mail there, but its stay is too short to give us opportunity to send replies to our letters by its return. When we hear from an Indian that the steamer is in, Mr. Willard puts up the mail and rushes over to get it on board the departing vessel. Whatever freight there may be for us is left at the cannery on our side of the river, and Mr. Willard has a trip of thirty miles with our little boat, the *Adeline*, to get it.

We have now at the canneries two towns in white tents. They employ several hundred white men. Most of our people are there, although Miss Matthews continues her school, and on Sabbath the services are well attended by the people coming over from the canneries.

We have been obliged to take two other children, a boy and a girl, into our family. Ned, the boy, is thirteen. His mother died when he was a baby. He is to be chief of the Ravens, to succeed Cla-not and Don-a-wok, and is a real rollicking, mischievous boy. His father, who idolizes his only child, has begged us, ever since we first came to Chilkat, to take Ned and make him a good man. You never saw a man so delighted when we did take the boy after our return from Sitka. He says "a long time his heart was only sick, but now all time glad because of Ned."

Ann is sixteen. Her mother died when Ann was a baby, and her father, old and almost blind, took for his second wife the daughter by a former husband of his first wife. So Ann's stepmother is her half sister. Ann came to me a year ago last winter and asked me to take her, saying that she wanted so much to be good, but could not be at home. She said that when she would try to pray before going to sleep, her sister-stepmother would poke her up, saying that she knew Ann was only asking God to kill the stepmother. It was impossible for us to take Ann at that time. I counseled her to be patient, that perhaps God meant her to lead her people to Him, and that after awhile He would open the way to a different life for her. She was afterward tempted to lead an evil life but said, when the miners came, that she had learned too much of God's word to willingly do wrong now.

This spring, when the people went to the canneries, she did not want to go, but she did not then ask us to take her. After a few days she came back, saying that she had seen so much evil that she was afraid. She wanted to be good: wouldn't we let her stay with us? Of course we could not refuse her request. She and the girl Fanny share one end of our spare room.

This seems particularly our work. The people love and confide in us, and it is a critical time in their history and that of this country. The people scarcely know where they are themselves, but, trusting us, they come and say, "You are our father and mother. You must tell us what to do with the white man. You must lead us like your little children."

Carrie M. Willard

DEAR FRIENDS: We have been having a soft rain for two or three days. It falls so lightly and gently and makes all things so beautiful that we have listened to its patter with grateful joy.

Our big, rollicking, handsome Indian boy Ned took the canoe yesterday and went out into the bay for fish and came in with a great stringful of the delicate flounder. We ate them for breakfast this morning, never dreaming of what they cost.

A little before dinner, as Ned lay on the floor beside the cradle, which he touched now and then for Baby Fred's comfort, there was a thumping on the kitchen door, which we had barred. Looking up, I saw our second chief, Cla-not, pounding on it. I told Ned to go and open the door. He did so, and in another instant I heard a rush, a scream, a thud, and I was out myself in time to see Ned being hurled about. When he had seen the powerful man's face, Ned jumped for the sitting room door, to get into a place of safety, but Cla-not was too swift and too strong for him.

I quickly tried to demand the chief's attention, but, seeing that he paid no more heed than to the wind, I laid my strength to Ned's in trying to drag him away and make Cla-not wait for a talk with Mr. Willard. Cla-not marched the boy out of the door, however, and threw him down. Mr. Willard at last heard the commotion and came to us with his calm strength. Walking close up to the angry man, a word was passed, and the boy was released. Ned quietly stole into the house behind Mr. Willard, who stood talking with Cla-not. It seems that Cla-not was punishing Ned for bringing on the rain, for he had heard from the boy who had accompanied Ned yesterday that the latter had killed a fish which it was a trouble to keep in the canoe by hitting it on the head with a stone, and thus gave cause for the continuance of the rain which is blessing the earth and bringing the berries to beautiful maturity.

I do trust that Ned and Paul, who are to succeed Cla-not, will have gained by that time much of the knowledge and love of Christ.

We have now three children in our home. Many of the big boys, who ought to be in school and could help us at garden work to supply the Home with vegetables for winter, while still learning something useful, have gone elsewhere—some to the cannery lately built across the bay.

JULY 16

Our mail did not come on the steamer. Mr. Willard waited till eleven at night for its arrival this side the river and then had his long tramp through forest, brush and swamp. As he came to the brush he heard a bear only a few yards from him. There are plenty of bears, and they can be seen almost any evening on the mountainside.

Dr. Corlies is at Juneau this summer and will look after our mail. Dr. Jackson's contract takes effect this month. The steamer has the mail contract to the other points and leaves our mail in Juneau. Dr. Corlies takes it from the office there and sends it by Indian canoe within a given time after the steamer's departure.

Chilkat Man Outfitted for a Trading Trip
(from A. Krause, *Die Tlingit Indianer*)

Those of our people who have not already left Haines for the canneries, with but few exceptions, are to leave this week for a wholesale trading raid on interior Indians, to be gone some three weeks. I think they must be realizing that their time will be short, for they are fitting out the older children with trading packs, while all the women have packs besides their babies.

This being the case, we expect as soon as possible to set off for Klukwan, the upper village, where Louis Paul and Tillie were. We have been anxious for their success and welfare ever since they came to this country. We gave them what slates we had, thinking that, as Louis Paul and Tillie were only beginning, they could use the slates to even better advantage than books, though we divided with them the books sent us. We also divided the Sunday school papers and provided them with blackboard, chalk and the handbell that Eva sent. We have shared our own clothes with them, and given of everything for their house we could think of. They have gone back to Wrangell by steamer. The experiment has been well tried; good has been done. The people have learned to want education and now will be more ready to receive it. The house put up for Louis is an excellent log house. By taking down the partition, we can make a good meeting house with a lodging room above, which we can use when we go to hold meetings and school.

AUGUST 7

We were aroused from sleep this morning by the only Indian woman in the village tapping on the window. She had been sent by three miners who were so nearly in a nude condition that they wished Mr. Willard to come down to them on the beach and if possible to give them some covering and food. They had not had a mouthful since yesterday morning and for four days had lived on only such berries as they could get and the small black mussels which the Indians regard as poisonous at this season of the year.

The men were covered and brought into the house—"home," as one of them said, where they were experiencing something of the delights which soldiers found when they came home from the war. These three had come from the interior where they had been since sometime in May.

When they were telling us of the hardships they had undergone, I said, "What men will go through for money! Some of our friends felt that it was a good deal for us to come to the Chilkat, but see how much more you endure for gold."

They had left behind four others who were unable to get farther than the headwaters of Taiya Inlet. One was an old man of sixty or seventy years. Mr. Willard is now busy getting some of the Indians off to bring the four down.

The returned men are young and vigorous yet still had to work to reach here. They had waded streams, the current taking them off their feet, sweeping them down the rapids. At last they found a canoe, hidden by other miners last spring, and used it, paddling against headwinds till one p.m. Exhausted and famished, they made the shore, drew the canoe above high water mark, lay down on the sand and slept.

When they awoke, they found they had been visited by so high a tide that their boat was gone and, from the strong wind, had no doubt been blown back to the head of the inlet. It was impossible to reach us by foot, so they were obliged to retrace their weary steps. They then found the truant boat back at their starting place, and now after four days' pulling, wading, and swimming, they are safely here with friends. The channel is quiet this morning, and Mr. Willard hopes to get the other starving men down before long. They had found gold paying from fifteen to twenty dollars a day, but it cost them twenty dollars a day to live.

A month ago the larger party divided, the seven hereto mentioned men came back, while another four went on with a boat to examine a quartz ledge on Pelly River. Those four will probably make their way to Fort Yukon and from there proceed by steamer to San Francisco. The three here say that should the others attempt to return this way, they will be overtaken by the snows and will have no food and no chance of reaching us alive.

Mr. Willard sent Ned flying to the Kinney cannery with a note to the foreman for men to go up the inlet. Mr. Willard just received reply that the workers are on a strike and the foreman can get no one but will send to the other side, where some men can probably be had.

The Indians are crazy to make money. Both canneries have stores, and prices have been brought down to fairness. At the same time, the prices of fish have run up so the Indians can make fifteen dollars a day fishing. What they are striking for now I do not know.

We were surprised a week ago last Sabbath to find, as the steamer arrived at the canneries, that Miss Rankin, assistant matron at Fort Wrangell, was aboard and had come to visit. She will stay till next steamer, which may arrive by another Sabbath. She and Miss Gould of Hydah came out last September with Miss Matthews and Dr. Jackson. Miss Rankin's visit is very refreshing.

AUGUST 8

Not being able to get Indians to help yesterday, Mr. Willard took the *Adeline,* with the three tired and sore miners, up the Taiya Inlet for the others. Just before they started, two Indians made an appearance and consented to go along. As these two were strong and understood pulling an oar, I felt much easier. The rescuers may not be back for ten days, in case of headwinds. But if all is fair, they may get back two days hence. Mr. Willard took provisions with him.

I am alone this morning with the babies. Miss Matthews and Miss Rankin are spending a day in the grand old pine woods. The boys are across the bay getting logs for steps to the beach and a boathouse. I sent the girls on an errand around the beach. They are all learning well. The girls are becoming helpful in the house—sweeping and chamber work, cooking and care of the kitchen. They do these things well for such young girls.

AUGUST 10

Mr. Willard got back with his crew in the night. They found the men living and in good spirits, considering that they had had nothing to eat for a week save two fish, a half a salmon they had found partially dried and decayed, and which made them sick, and two fish which they shot and managed in some way to get out of the water. They did not dare to eat more than half a fish at a time, lest they could get no more. They seemed very grateful for the help Mr. Willard brought them. They told how, when so weary, they encouraged one another with "Never mind, boys. If we can hold out till we get to the missionary's, we'll be all right. It's like home there." And they did hold out till the next day without a morsel to eat.

AUGUST 27

I must give you an idea of how we live.

One week Ann takes the kitchen, cooking, washing dishes, baking, etc.; Fanny the sweeping, chamber work, etc. At week's end, they switch.

In the morning—say Monday, for instance—while Fanny makes herself neat for the getting of breakfast, Ann gives the living rooms a cleaning and brightening up. Miss Matthews joins Fanny in the kitchen, and together they get breakfast on the table in the dining room. By the time I have washed and dressed the babies, the Indian children's breakfast is set in the kitchen. They eat at the same time we do, always giving thanks and asking the blessing with bowed heads. After the meal Ann takes up the crumbs and goes to her chamber work, while Fanny washes the dishes and tidies the kitchen. Ned saws wood.

All being through their tasks together, they then have their study hours. After recitations with Miss Matthews in reading, writing, spelling and arithmetic, the Bible lesson, singing and prayer, I get dinner with Fanny. She and Ann together do up the dishes, then proceed to wash the soiled clothing of the week. Then I get supper for all by the time they have the clothes in the last rinse water. After supper the girls scour table and floor, making the kitchen shine. Then we have family prayers and go to bed.

The routine is varied as circumstances indicate. On another day comes the ironing, which the girls do together. I have Ned and Ann's little brother, Adam, who is with us a good deal, wear starched white and calico shirts on purpose to teach the girls laundrying. They have learned to do them up nicely. Another day they have baking, and they can bake excellent bread. Then they have sewing. I teach them to cut and fit their own clothing, and they have learned to sew on the machine better than most girls of their ages at home. Last week I had them learning pants making—real "American pants"—and knitting. They each have knit woolen stockings for themselves. They go berrying and fishing and make a happy crew.

There are many items of interest in connection with them that I wish I could tell you. I have rushed along into this subject because I was so troubled at your distress for us that I wished to set your minds at rest. We are doing and will do just what the Father puts into our hands and try to trust results of what we do, with all that we cannot do, to Him. Even now we believe that we are seeing evidences of His blessings with our children here and with some of our people.

We have been trying to beautify our mission home. After making Miss Matthews' room the best in the house, Mr. Willard and I went to the study. We had concluded that our bedroom downstairs was not a healthful place, especially for the little ones. It would make a more convenient study and office for Mr. Willard than the room he has had upstairs. So we made the change.

Fanny sewed up the house lining (for it is not plastered) of unbleached cheesecloth, as Ann had done for Miss Matthews' room, and we put it on the walls with a narrow strip of turkey red for the border. You wouldn't believe what a pretty effect it made. All the carpet I could put together was not enough, but in Miss Matthews' Christmas box from home was a piece of red and black linsey-woolsey, which she gave me as a border. I had also some thin red flannel, which I cut into two straight curtains and hung on a carved Indian totem stick for the window toward the bay. Then we have a long shelf with red lambrequin for bric-a-brac, and underneath a long bright cushioned box for settee and to hold bedclothing.

The study is more unique. The floor is covered with fur robes. The walls are rough board. There is a cross-legged table of Mr. Willard's manufacture covered with green oilcloth, as are also the chairs, bookcase and medicine case. The latter is a cracker box set upright on legs, stained dark brown, with the lock and hinges of brass. On its long door I painted a scene of water tumbling down over gray stones among flowers, ferns and moss. Across the corner stands my easel. On the wall hangs an ornamented squirrel robe. Crossed above it are two Indian bows, and from them, hanging over the robe, a quiver of arrows. Then there is a camp chair, and a black bearskin lined with red flannel on the floor. In front of the table lies a marmot robe on which stands the study chair, covered with another squirrel robe.

Willard

At one side of the window next the bay is the gunshop. A box holding the ammunition is covered with a skin and on its top is a huge stone washbowl, given us by Shat-e-ritch as a valuable relic. In it, on a small mink skin, stand the guns—rifle and shotgun—leaning, at the top, into the arms of polished deer horns that Mr. Willard mounted on yellow cedar. From branches of the horns hang the Colt's revolver and its Apache belt given him by a miner, and Mr. Willard's own revolver brought from home. Scattered about on the walls are sketches of Alaska scenery in oil, and the painting of *The Virgin of Light* with the plaster foot. A very good bust of Shakespeare, given us by a friend, looks down from among the books.

For outdoor exercise, I have taken Kotzie and the Indian children and worked on both the Home lots and our own. We have made a gravel walk from the porch down to the beach, with two flights of terrace steps. It remains to be finished to the schoolhouse. We have beautiful house plants—calla lily, roses, geraniums, heliotrope, fuchsias, etc.—which have bloomed profusely.

We have eaten Indian apples this summer— the queerest fruits, about the size of red haws and looking like them; but the seed is like the quince, and they taste like tiny green apples. I do think that grafts would grow and bud on them.

SEPTEMBER 3

Among the myths of the Tlingits is one about the owl. In a conversation with some of the children and young people one day, I said, "But then you know that owls cannot talk."

172

"Oh," was the reply, "they can't talk 'Merican; that's why the snow-people think they say nothing. Just Tlingit they speak, and all the Tlingits know what they say. Snow-people say no witches in Chilkat, but Chilkat Tlingit see plenty witches."

"Then what is an owl?" I inquired.

"Bad spirit."

"What do they do?"

"Oh, plenty bad; no good 'tall. All Indians much 'fraid owl. He talk bad to everybody; no good words in him. He big thief too. Some nights plenty big Indian in house. Old owl come close by in dark pine tree. He talk bad. All Indians run out house to drive him away, 'cause he tell somebody going to die. Owl knows everything, but he big coward. He plenty 'fraid big Indian. Just young ones he strong take. Little woman, boy, go out by self—big owl turn him's heart upside down."

Two Sabbaths ago we had a sermon on witchcraft. After the service many of the younger people were gathered in the kitchen watching my preparations for dinner. On Saturday, Ned had neglected to split and house his wood until it had gotten quite damp in the rain; so that I had quite a tedious time getting the pot to boil, and I had occasion to look into it again and again.

"What is the matter with it?" I asked. I raised the lid again with all looking at me as I did so. I assumed an expression first of surprise, then, as I peered into the depths of the unmanageable fluid, my eyes became fixed and staring, opening wider and wider. With mouth also agape, I uttered the one startling word "Witches!" The Indians were watching with keen interest, and as their bodies, almost unconsciously, arose and followed their gaze, they looked with me into the pot that would not boil. Then, relaxing, I dropped the lid and told them that the witch I had seen was Ned's neglect to get the wood in dry. He had left it in the rain until it was wet and that made the wood so that I could not get a good fire; no boil in the pot. Then I told them there had been a time when the white people—my own forefathers—believed that witches kept the pot from boiling. When they had learned better to understand, when they had studied into God's ways—into the whys of things—they knew that witchcraft was nothing but foolishness. They had been a great many years in finding out the reasons for things that showed them the foolishness of witches. The good people did not wish the Indians to walk in darkness so long and that was the reason of our coming to teach them what we had had to find out. They might learn fast if they would but believe the good words.

Philip, the young silversmith, has long been a source of wonder and joy to us. Such earnest attention he has seemed to pay to every effort of ours to instruct him! He has a sad history, and once, on a trip from the interior, almost lost his life. His intelligence and indomitable pluck barely saved him, but he lost all his toes and all the flesh from his hands. They are but bits of drawn-up bones. Yet he does beautiful work in silver, and not only that, but works at anything he can get when he does not have orders for carving. We have had him employed a good part of the summer in putting up the boat-house and in making shakes for a wood and vegetable house. He said that he would rather work for the minister than make money at the canneries, because the white men there seemed to care only about making money. He wanted to make money, but he wanted to take care of his soul too, and he knew that the minister cared for his soul. It was he who surprised me one evening during our first winter here by remarking to me that I was not lonesome because my books talked to me like friends. We have felt that he was very near the kingdom of God—that he was following the truth so far as he knew it. Imagine, then, our distress, our grief and surprise, when, a week or two ago, we heard he had taken another wife. We heard this at almost the same time that news came of his rejoicing over the birth of his first baby girl. He came himself to tell us how glad he was when his daughter was born. He wanted her to be "all 'Merican baby," he said, and not even to have an Indian name. He wanted us to have the baby and to teach her. He wished me to give her an American name, and he wanted Baby Fred's nursing bottle for her.

But through all Philip's expressions of happiness my heart was aching with keenness of sorrow for his wrongdoing. So, after we had all sympathized with him and his heart was largely unburdened, I drew him away to the sitting room, where, seating myself near him, I said,

"Philip, my heart is very, very sick."

He looked into my face with such clear and questioning eyes so full of pained wonder that I almost hoped to find the report of his offense all a mistake, but I went on:

Willard

"You know how, a long, long time ago, you told us the story of your life; of your long, hard journey to the north country; of your struggles with terrible storms in going down the awful snowslides; of the big waves that dashed your canoe to splinters and hurled you against the great walls of rock; then of how you seemed to die in the blackness of the waters, and at last how, God having brought you back to life, you found yourself in the world again, though your body was partly dead. And then you told how you came slowly and painfully back to the village where you had left the wife and baby for whose sakes you had risked and suffered so much. But when you staggered to the house you found that another had taken your place. I remember, too, how you longed to die—how you wished that you had died in that fearful mountain gulch and how the months dragged on till the unfaithful wife left with her child to lead a life in Sitka, and the world rose up new for you again, and you took the faithful and loving Leah for your wife. Do you remember how good and pure and true you said she was, and how you loved her? It made us so glad to know that. Old things having passed away, you two were true to each other and trying together to serve the God who had so strangely spared you. Our hearts were always glad in thinking of you, because we thought you were trying to walk in the right way; and now we have heard that you have taken another wife—that you have Leah and her sister too. Is it true?"

He had not lifted his eyes from my face while I was speaking. When I asked the question, his countenance did not change, only a fresh wonder came into it, and he said, "Why, have you only just heard of it? I took Mollie a moon and a half ago."

I could only say, "Oh Philip, how could you? You know that God forbids such things?"

With new surprise quickening his sensitive face, he asked, "What is that, Nauk-y-stih?"

"Don't you know that God's word says one wife for one man and one husband for one woman?"

There was eager pain in the wonder now as he glanced across to the Bible which lay on the table. Following the suggestion, I opened it and read to him the holy law of marriage. Leaning forward in his eagerness, it seemed as though he must almost bring the words from the book before I could utter them.

When I had finished, several moments passed before he spoke. I could see that his heart was beating fast, and his eyes were dim as they bent on the book. At length, raising his head and looking at me earnestly, he cleared his throat and said, "Oh mother, why did I never hear God's word before? Now for the first time, I hear His law. If I know His way before, I never have any wife but Leah. My heart is sick. Wait. I can't see which way my face is turned." And he hurriedly left the room.

When he reentered, perhaps half an hour later, my husband had joined me. I told Mr. Willard how matters stood. We were talking it over seated side by side when Philip walked in, his face showing the manly determination which could hardly find expression in his rather limping gait, and took his stand opposite us. After wiping the damp from his forehead, he said, in a studied but earnest way, "Mr. Willard and Nauk-y-stih, you are my father and mother. You always do me good. Now I do wrong. I take two wives. I never hear God's word about it before. I thank you, my mother, for reading it to me. My heart is sick. I love no woman besides Leah. If I know God's word before, I shut my arms tight around her and let no one else come in. But I tell you how it was. I wanted to take no more wife, but Leah's sister was ready to be married. The boy who was to take her wouldn't. He would say, 'Wait. Wait! Wait till after Sunday. Till another moon.' Then all knew he didn't mean to take her at all. Many Indians have two wives, so the friends say to me, 'You take her. You take her.' And by and by I do. I have her now one moon and a half and don't know it's bad. Now I know the good way. I take only Leah for my wife, but I must not take this poor girl by the shoulder and say, 'Get you gone! Quick!' I brought her in. I must not give her shame. I will tell her, 'Sit down awhile in my house easy. By and by go out without much tongues and shame.'"

We commended his compassion and bid him carry out his plan, with earnest prayer for them all.

Raven is the Chilkat's supreme being. He is the creator and preserver of all things, for not only did he make the world, but upon his wings it is borne. The end of the world will come when he flies from under it. And not only is Raven the power almighty, but he is the power almighty for evil. The people must appease Raven. His sufferance of them they must propitiate by sacrifices.

A conversation between our Indian girl Bessie Ann Frazer (who must have been about fourteen years old when it took place) and an older Indian was reported to me the other day by a third person, who had been much interested in their discussion in regard to the claims of the new religion. John had asserted his full belief in the doctrines of his fathers.

Ann responded by saying, "I used to believe Raven made the world. But when the minister came and told us about his God and showed God's book, and I learned to read his words my self, I no more believe in Raven. Now, if you want me to believe in Raven, show me Raven's book..."

SEPTEMBER 10

While we were at breakfast a Native man came and asked me if he might bake some bread in our stove. I told him *yes*, if he would bring it quickly, before my fire went down. He returned to the village, and directly another man came carrying a sack of flour, his wife bearing a big bowl in which to mix the bread and a package of sugar. They were going to have a feast. The people of the three lower villages were invited, and our people wanted to bake up this sack of flour into flat sugar cakes.

The man did the mixing with his wife looking on. He took out a bowl of flour, put just as little water in it as would make dough so stiff that he pounded and hammered it, in pugilistic fashion, with his double fist. Sprinkling a little sugar on the lump occasionally and a spoonful of water, the pounding would be resumed, until at last we were obliged to insist on its being put into the oven. Reluctantly he seemed to flatten it out, but at last the cakes were panned, put in to bake, and the man's wife sent home with the flour. He stayed to mind the baking, which took about one hour with fire in the stove and another hour without any.

The next arrival was a man who wanted to buy sacks of beans and of rice for the same feast. Three friends were giving it jointly. We had none to sell him, so he was obliged to go to the canneries.

Then came a woman to borrow a washtub to hold the beans and rice when they were cooked, for this was the day of preparation for the feast. The cooking utensils were small, except for the great baskets in which the people cook by means of redhot stones dropped into the mixture that they wish to boil. In this case a large quantity was to be cooked in small portions.

Then the tub was wanted for the great central dish, from which the totem dishes of the guests could be filled. They often carry their own dishes and spoons, each carved elaborately with their family totem, or coat-of-arms. For instance, suppose a man is of the Owl family, of the Kogwanton tribe. He will probably have a dish ornamented with owl carvings and a horn spoon whose handle represents the cinnamon bear, or a commingling of the two in one. They have many styles of dishes in wood, horn and stone, with carved decorations. The arrangement of the ever-varying and ever-recurring totem is curious, sometimes grotesque, and often graceful in design.

At their feasts these great dishes and spoons, valuable and handed down through generations as is our great grandmother's china at home, are gathered about by a group of the same family and

Carved Spoons

filled by the master of the feast from the central dish. This is similar to the custom among home people when refreshments are served to groups of guests at small tables from the main dining table. However, the Chilkats are more social, as each partakes from this common totem dish with his own spoon. These spoons are large enough to answer for individual dishes. They usually hold from half a pint to a pint. Some will hold as much as a quart and look like gourd ladles.

Finally, one of the hosts came to buy calico to tear up and give away at the *co-ek-y*, or the great gift-giving prelude to the feast which would take place that night, a feast for the dead. Of course we would not give him calico for such a purpose.

SEPTEMBER 10

We had thirty-five or forty at church yesterday. The people left the canneries and still are feasting. Next month the medicine man Kaht-lutl is to give a great feast on the completion of a

181

house he has been building for three years in memory of his dead in Y'hin-da-stachy.

Canoes are coming daily from below—Juneau, Sitka, Hoonah and Fort Wrangell—to get salmon at the upper village. These people say they have been standing all summer waiting for the fish to come, but in all they had gotten but forty dried. Winter is coming on, and they have been unable to make provision for it. Usually they have by this season great storehouses full of dried salmon and salmon oil, not only enough for themselves, but for trade with the lower tribes. I fear there will be trouble for them this winter. If it were not for the babies, whose frequent illnesses require every care and comfort that we can give them here, I would be eager to go to the upper village for the winter and, indeed, may find it necessary to go.

I heard yesterday the story of the owl's origin as believed by all the Tlingit tribes: At Sitka an old blind woman lived with her son and his wife. It was a time of great scarcity of goods. The son went every day to hunt and fish, but could get nothing. He and the old mother barely kept soul and body together with the few roots and berries that could be found. But the young wife thrived well—upon what, no one knew. In the night when the old woman would wake up from sleep, she would say to her daughter-in-law, "What have you got there to eat?"

"Nothing."

"Oh yes! I smell fish. I hear the oil dropping on the fire."

"No you don't. There's nothing to eat."

Again the hungry old woman would say,

"What are you eating? You have fish. I hear you eating it."

"No," came the answer.

The truth was, according to the story, that having the power of a witch, the young woman went every midnight to the rocks overhanging the sea, and there, with tree branches which she swayed back and forth and crossed and recrossed before her, she charmed the young herring from their haunts. They flung themselves from the waves to the rocks at her feet. Gathering them into her basket, she would take them home, string them (as is their custom still) on a stick, which was then fastened into the earth at an inclining angle under which the house fire was built. After roasting the herring, she would have a good meal and sleep again.

Matters went on in this way until one night when the husband was away, the old mother's questioning angered her daughter-in-law so much that, snatching a fish from the stick, she tore out the burning entrails and cried out, "Hold out your hand then. You shall have some." She forcibly closed the old fingers around the hot mass until the palm was deeply burned.

When the husband came home the next day, he asked what made his mother cry so. His wife said she didn't know. Determined to hear from his mother herself, he said to his wife, "I am going hunting again. Go you to the woods and get me bark lining (to tie on arrowheads) for my arrow."

While the wife was gone, the old woman told him all her troubles, and he at once decided what to do. When his wife returned with the bark strings, he took his bow and put off in his canoe as though he were going a distance. But as soon as he had turned the point of land which hid him from the view of the village, he drew the canoe ashore. He hid it in the bushes and secreted himself until after nightfall. When the moon began to rise, he stole toward the village and, taking a station which would command a view of the beach, there awaited developments.

At midnight he saw in the moonlight the figure of his wife approaching the scene of her nightly incantation. He watched her through it all and followed softly to the house, where he saw her cook and eat the fish and deny his mother's cry for food. Then he returned to his canoe. The next day he caught a hair seal and, taking it home, made his wife eat so much of its fat that she fell into a deep sleep, so deep, indeed, that the midnight hour had passed when she was aroused by her husband's command to go to the canoe and carry up the fish he had just brought home. He, having stolen her art, had himself used it and filled his canoe with herring while she slept. She went to the canoe and sat down on the beach. Her voice came feebly as she called to her husband to bring the baskets. He would not, and she would not go for them. So she sat on the sand all day.

As the moon arose she started toward the mountain, intending to follow a gulch to its top. But when she came to the great stone which stands opposite the gate of the Sheldon Jackson Institute, she sat down and immediately turned into an owl. It is for this reason, then, that the owl works in the night and talks in the moonlight.

Mrs. Dickinson
(from A. Krause, *Die Tlingit Indianer*)

SEPTEMBER 27

Mr. Willard and Miss Matthews and Mrs. Dickinson are at the upper villages this week. The girls and babies remain at home with me.

This has been a specimen day and, as the little ones are all asleep, I will run over its events. There has not been an outside Indian near the house, owing to the great annual feast at Y'hin-da-stachy, but we are always busy. We arose at seven o'clock this morning, got breakfast over, the

185

little ones ready, and the Saturday cleaning and preparation done. Then, putting Fred in a comfort, I sat him in his cart, gave Kotzie her shovel, and led the girls with two larger shovels and the wheelbarrow to digging clods and banking up the house for winter. Anyone else who might help us with this work, even Ned, has run off to the feast.

The girls went at it with a will and we got it almost done. While we were working in the front of the house, one of the girls screamed out that the boat's ways were floating off. And there, sure enough, going rapidly out with the tide was the log roadway which had been worked on for so many weary days. I feared it might get out into the channel's current and be carried utterly away. I knew that it would be next to impossible to replace it by a new one this year, and the *Adeline* was at anchor in the bay, but must be housed for the winter. How could it be done without these ways and pulleys?

So, laying Fred on his back in the comfort, I pulled on my rubber boots, snatched up the keys and, calling to the girls to follow me, ran to the boathouse and got out ropes and paddles while the girls ran the canoe down the beach. Springing into the shell, we were off on the water. Fanny sat high and dry in the prow, Ann in the stern, both working hard while I with my ropes sat amidships. We reached the logs, roped them in and tugged them back to the *Adeline*. Boarding the white beauty, I tied the ropes securely to her prow, and we were soon ashore again.

Poor little ones left behind! Kotzie had followed to the water's edge as Fred cried himself to sleep. We ate dinner and after evening singing, Bible lesson and prayer, I took the children up to bed. When they were snugly tucked in, I heard noises on the beach like the landing of a boat. Looking out, I could just distinguish a canoe being hauled up and a figure coming up the path to the house. I heard the voices of white men.

As the solitary figure was about to pass to the back of the house, I called out from the window, "Who is there?"

"A party from the interior. We heard that you were here and tried hard to get here tonight."

I told him that Mr. Willard was not at home, but that I would be down in a minute and would most gladly give them anything they needed.

They were not in the pitiable state of the former party of miners, but they were tired and hungry. They are now comfortably housed in the schoolhouse with fire and provisions, and the day has almost passed for me.

OCTOBER 9

Our itinerants returned, holding service two weeks ago at Klukwan, last Sabbath at Y'hin-da-stachy. I had a congregation here of twenty.

The feasting had at last ended, and the people were en route for Chilkoot to put up salmon. They said, "The days are dear now because so few will be before the big snows." But they stopped for church, and we had a good time. I can get on now very well without an interpreter.

The mail brought us a telegram from Dr. Kendall, saying, "Go on with the building." We would shrink from this undertaking but believe that we will be so directed as to secure more glory to His name. We are grateful for this authority. Philip and Sarah, with Adeline, were here on Sabbath. Monday Philip went to work on getting out logs for the Home. Last evening, he towed in and landed the first eight logs for the building. Taking the children to the beach, I sat down on a fallen tree and watched the landing. I forgot my weariness in the joy of seeing a beginning of this house, so labored for, prayed for and waited for. Every bump of the logs sent a throb of gratitude through me, and I felt penitent for my want of faith a few weeks ago. I am now glad and thankful!

OCTOBER 11

Yesterday morning Philip came early, looking as though he had lost his last friend.

"Me baby sick. Me *min-ten* (little) baby sick," he said. "Me no sleep last night."

"What is the matter?" I asked. "Did Baby cry?"

"No. No cry. Me heart too sick baby."

I sent him to bring Adeline and her mother and soon found the baby quite sick with lung fever. The people's houses are shut up during the wet summer, while the roofs are open, letting in all the rain on the earthen floors. When they bring a few pieces of bark for floors, the people go right into the houses, build a fire and breathe in the mold and must seeping out of the ground and walls.

After a day of much nursing and care, Adeline breathed better and seemed in a fair way to recover if the care could be continued. We still have the family of three here in the coziest corner of the sitting room.

Chilkat Woman Sewing

As I have clothed Adeline in flannel now, I asked her mother to give me the garment I took off so I could show you a specimen of the Indian women's sewing. This is the style of dress worn by every Chilkat female, big and little. But in the case of the women, there is more often a straight gathered skirt worn over the dress and perhaps a cotton jacket. The clothes are all, even when made of the flimsiest material, sewed with such extreme nicety! Their favorite position for sewing is lying on the floor, face downward and elbows resting on the ground. They hold the needle between thumb and finger, pointing outward.

OCTOBER 16

Philip's baby is dead. The body is to be cremated today at Chilkoot, whither its mother and her friends took it yesterday at daybreak.

The baby had improved. When on Saturday Philip told me that he would take Adeline home at noon, I told him it would be best, as she was better. The weather had grown milder and quiet, and their house had been thoroughly heated, their friends having kept up a constant fire for several days. He went down and hung up thick blankets, making a warm room for Adeline and her mother. They wrapped the child well in blankets (it was dressed in my baby's flannels and socks) and took her down to the village. Early yesterday morning Philip came to tell us that the baby was gone. His slow step, white face and swollen eyes told something of his grief. We too had become attached to this baby and were much grieved.

As soon as Adeline was dead, friends began to wrap her body in blankets, ready for the mysterious journey to the spirit world. They ran out a canoe and put the baby into it with her mother and hurried away to Chilkoot, in spite of the father's agonized entreaties. He did not believe that the child was dead. He begged them to not take her on the Sabbath but wait till Monday.

They left him alone. He came to tell us, saying that if his child were dead, he would go away on the steamboat to work. Adeline was truly his idol. Never have I seen anywhere more tender solicitude, anxious love and earnest, watchful care, than he showed to his baby. He had this summer, with part of his earnings, bought a camphor wood trunk and kept several lovely rose blankets in it. When the baby took sick, he immediately opened his treasure trunk and made her bed more comfortable than I could have by giving him my best.

While here, he would throw himself on his hands and knees beside his baby on the floor and lay his head on her pillow, cooing to her and kissing her like the tenderest mother. He was the baby's best nurse and would not leave her all those days of her sickness except to get their food. But he rested when I took her. When I came at night, whether at twelve or two or four o'clock, and took up the babe into my arms, after seeing her comfortably settled, he would draw out from about his head somewhere his book and begin to pore over it, appealing to me constantly for confirmation or correction of what he had spelled. He seemed so troubled about the burning of the body. We told him to let them burn it, that doing so could not make the little one unhappy, but that we wished him to make no feast nor burning or tearing up of food and clothing. He said he would have to burn two blankets with the baby and give her tribe food, but he would do no more.

Now everyone is gone again. Some have gone to Chilkoot for the cremation. The majority, however, have gone to Klukwan for another great feast given to the lower villages in return compliment.

Some of the lower people, who had raised bushels of potatoes and used them for the Y'hinda-stachy feast, have not one morsel of food for winter, and they have families of children. They intended going to work on the dog salmon last week to dry it, but now comes the call to feast at Klukwan with the Kogwantons.

Ned has never come back since going to the feast...

Carrie M. Willard

Willard

DEAR FRIENDS: Let me take this opportunity of thanking you all for your interest in the boat. We did not get a steamer but a good row-and-sail boat which answers our purposes well and is a great comfort. We have built a log boathouse on the beach, where between trips she is safely sheltered.

During these summer months the steamers come to the canneries which are on the Chilkat Inlet. The distance from Haines is two or three miles across the peninsula through a terrible trackless bush. We have no roads in this country, you know, and to go around the point, as we must for our freight, it is thirty miles. So you see even now how much we need the boat. Then for six months during the winter I suppose there will be no steamer and our only dependence from Juneau will be our own little boat.

REV. AND MRS. P. F. SANBORNE, DEAR FRIENDS: There is something so good to write! Last evening the first eight logs for the Home were towed in and delivered above high tide by Philip, our silversmith. It brings a feeling akin to that experienced upon hearing of the first gift toward the building (a year and a half ago).

You write to know what to do for us. We shall need everything in the spring. We hope to get the logs on the ground ready for early work when the snow goes off.

We will be obliged to take some boys before we have the house up, in order to secure them and that we may have their help in the work to be done. We can do this by using the schoolhouse as a temporary dormitory. But as yet, we have no boys' clothing nor bedticks nor blankets. Of the clothing, the very best kind will be of brown ducking canvas—at least for pantaloons—and blue denims or hickory for waists and shirts. The latter might be varied with strong jeans and cheviot flannel. Our Ned can wear a pair of new jean pantaloons only one month before they need new seat and knees. This clothing should be for boys of ages ranging from ten to sixteen. Our beds will for the most part be single ones—say two widths of hickory two yards long, with a six-inch strip between them for the thickness of the bed. Blankets, colored ones, are better than quilts and more easily kept clean than comforts. They are cheaper, it is said, on this coast than in the East. Then we shall want crash towels and everything. May God bless you for your good words!

Carrie M. Willard

CHILCAT MISSION
HAINES, ALASKA
OCTOBER 17, 1883

DEAR MRS...: In a note by our last mail but one, Mrs. L. asked me to write you in reference to our Chilkat children and select for you a girl to name. I gladly comply at my earliest opportunity, and yet I can only write in a general way. I am not able at once to give you a particular child. We most fondly hope to have the Home open by another summer, and it is exceedingly desirable that the support of its children shall all have been secured by that happy day. However, knowing the difficulties as well as appreciating the wish of those who give to this purpose that neither change nor failure should be connected with the name the givers choose for the child they sponsor, I think delay of appointment better than risk of a greater disappointment.

You cannot understand just what the difficulties are; they are legion. Every superstition of the people, every tie, interferes with the plans of missionaries. I might give you a promising girl brought by her mother today. I might take her into my family, adopting her for you with all papers and ceremonies for the transference. Yet before our mail is ready to go, taking to you an account of proceedings and probabilities, I might have to write you the account of her leaving or being taken away by her family or given as a wife. I might give her the name you chose and let the family and her go away, leaving me with the assurance that the child would be ready when I can take her, and then the next week find that the family has removed elsewhere, from whence I could not ever expect to receive the girl.

So I assure you, dear friends, that from such a point of view, these scholarships are trying and discouraging. You wish to watch the growth and progress of a particular child. But is this best? May I not suggest what may be a better plan?— one which will both enlarge the sympathies of the

givers and their experimental knowledge of mission work and relieve the missionaries of so great
a tax. Instead of saying, "Select for us a child of
good promise—one we can keep and whose course
we can follow—and we will support her in your
school and call her 'So-and-So,'" suppose you
should say, "We wish to have a *scholarship* in
your school, to be named 'So-and-So,' and would
be glad to have occasional accounts of the child
who may be benefitted by it. And suppose you pay
your one hundred dollars a year into the hand of
the Board of Home Missions for this scholarship,
always to be known by your chosen name. Then,
if for any cause it became necessary to substitute
any other child for the one first selected, you
might in this way gain the histories of a dozen
children, with all the varied circumstances that
cause the change. In this way you would learn of
the circumstances that cause changes and thus
learn more of the habits and needs of the
Chilkats than you could in any other way. You
might have the same child for a number of years,
but if not, you would have the joy of knowing that
more than one little candle had been lighted.

Have you heard of the child-wife in our school?
Her husband is sawing wood for us today. He
sometimes comes to school with her and his own
children, whom she lugs with her everywhere she
goes. It is almost two years since he took her as
his wife. She is the daughter of his brother and is
not over eleven years old now. She has fretted so
that her father has several times allowed her to
come home for awhile. She is with her parents
just now, and her father says he does not want

her to go back to her husband. "She cries too much," her father says. He wants us to take her into the Home, and oh, I do hope he will not change his mind before the place is ready for her.

That bright son of Shat-e-ritch who so manfully helped to take our mission stuff up the river a year ago and whom we hoped to have in the Home, has fallen heir to his uncle-chief's houses, blankets and widow—an old woman from whom death may release him in a few years, but he has taken possession and is now master of a chief's estate...

        Carrie M. Willard

CHILKAT MISSION
HAINES, ALASKA
NOVEMBER 7, 1883

DEAR FRIENDS: Our Fanny does the most of the interpeting now and does it well, though it is trying. When we found that Mrs. Dickinson was not coming last Sabbath, Mr. Willard said, "Well, Fanny will have to talk for me today."

She looked down and did not make any reply except a movement of impatience or uneasiness. Mr. Willard began to go over the lesson with her—on the raising of the widow's son of Nain. When he was through, he asked if she understood.

"No," she said distinctly.

I called her to come and sit down beside me in the big window and, taking a lot of blocks from Kotzie's play box, I built a city with a wall about it, explained the purpose of the latter, then showed the little house where lived the widow, told her of one boy who cared for her, of his death, of her grief. With a doll and the lid of a box and a winding ribbon, we led the procession of mourners down the street and through the city's gate. We had before seen that Jesus was leaving a neighboring town and now was nearing the gate as the funeral came out. Then the joyful return.

Among the many applications, I spoke of how like the dead we all are, of our helplessness until we are touched by Him who makes us strong. There was an instant change in her whole aspect ...and I knew then that she would do well. She did do well, speaking out with perfect ease.

We had two services, and a room full of children followed us home at nightfall. I had asked Minnie, the child-wife to come home with me because I wanted to have a talk with her. But, as all the rest came and the room filled up, I concluded to give them all the benefit of the lesson meant at first for her. I preached them a brief sermon full of questions on the commandments, and the hymns were sung joyously. The children are learning to sing beautifully together and are getting quite an idea of the parts, trying, with no mean success, the alto and bass as well as the air.

Minnie's father came to see us about her. He says that his brother is angry that he didn't send her back. The brother says that she belongs to him and he needs her. I told her father that if he did make her go back again, I should tell the man-of-war the very first thing when I see it again.

Oh, if we only had the Home! Or if we had known in time that we could have gotten provision enough for more. Then how glad we would have been to lay it in and take these children!

Willard

Among the demands of yesterday, besides my home and children, was the cutting and fitting of a black alpaca polonaise for Mrs. Chilkoot Jack. She has a tall, slender figure, a sweet young face, and a good head with a heavy braid of glossy black hair, and in her new dress looks like a lady.

Before I had finished cutting the dress came Mrs. Harry Kah-dum-jah, a crippled woman with four children (two of whom I immediately dispatched to school), with an old frock coat which her husband had gotten from some of the white men. She wanted a whole suit from it for her five-year-old boy. We ripped it up and cut a jacket from the skirts and a pair of pants from the sleeves. From the extravagent pleasure at the result, I could see that she had not really expected me to give her all she wanted out of that coat. She is bright and a good seamstress and readily took up all my directions for the outfit's making. When she had finished sewing the seams, and I brought a hot flatiron to press them out, she seemed as much delighted as if I had presented her with a new tailor-made suit.

The boy himself was so rejoiced with the idea of having a coat that fitted him that he ran off to school with the body of it on while we were fixing the sleeves. Her baby boy is a little older than mine—a beautiful child just creeping about the floor. He had only the customary short cotton shirt about his shoulders—though it was so cold that with all the fire I could keep going in the big box stove, I dared not let my own baby down on the floor, even with all his thick warm flannels.

Her baby was not well. When I brought an old pair of flannel drawers to put on him, his mother showed me that his spine was curved.

"Why, what did that?" I asked.

She said, "Witches."

I had many times seen the child lugged about by a six-year-old sister, slung over her back in a blanket. I gave the mother a lesson on witchcraft and the proper care of not only babies but their weak sisters.

Before I had finished, as if to give the discourse point, my baby Fred, in his healthy restlessness, grew tired of the armchair into which I had tucked him. Trying to gain the floor, he reached it in too much haste and got such a bump on his wee pug nose as brought the blood. As soon as I had hushed him in my arms, I turned to the woman with an expression of great concern and asked, "What is the matter with the baby's nose? See the blood!"

She looked surprised and answered that he struck it when he fell from the chair. But I gravely said, "It must be witches."

She glanced quickly up to my face. I could see the expression of half terror, half surprise that had possession of her before her searching eyes revealed to her the changing expression of mine. Then we broke into a hearty laugh as she clearly comprehended my meaning.

There were a dozen or more minor calls from men about wood, women who were in trouble with their husbands, parents wanting us to take their children, and counsels about a boy who ran away and may have fled into the woods. Then came the getting of dinner for the school-goers, the earlier lunching of Kotzie and Fred, and the putting of the latter to bed for his midday sleep.

After dinner the room was still full of Indians wanting help in various ways. Some had sick children whom they wished me to visit. It was impossible for me to leave home even for a moment until my own children were asleep in their beds for the night and their papa in the house to harken should they cry.

In the evening I took the lantern and went to the village. Ann and Fanny had washed up the dishes and wanted to go with me, so I gladly took them. We went to a little sick girl first. I found her lying curled up on a sheepskin spread on the floor near the fire. Her soft, large eyes looked mournfully out from her thick hair. Her quivering mouth was almost hidden by the blanket she drew tightly about her, but she saw the cakes I slipped under it and looked up at me as I stroked back her hair and sang her hymns in Tlingit. There were about thirty persons in the house. Some were at work, others idling, while a great fish, a yard long and nearly a foot thick, hung before a blazing fire on a string from the rafter above. An old man with a stick kept it spinning around. A pan beneath caught drippings. The people, old and young, joined in the singing. Then we repeated the twenty-third psalm in Tlingit. Her mother said the girl's most frequent cry was for "school." I gave directions for her care and this morning sent clean clothes and medicine.

Our next call was on an old Chilkoot doctor who lingers so strangely. He has been dying with consumption for years and now is blind. He caught my hand eagerly and between gasps for breath called me his mother, his grandmother, the good chief lady, etc., saying that he had wanted so much to see my face. I spoke to him of death, of God, the Savior and heaven. I told him the story of Paul, whom God made blind to outside things because He wished to open the eyes of his heart. We prayed. He professed to believe and asked me to cut his hair, saying that he wanted to die right and wished Mr. Willard to bury his body.

This house was also full of people listening to the good words. But time fails me now to tell of other visits. All were, I trust, profitable and will leave behind some blessing.

Carrie M. Willard

Afterword

Carrie M. Willard and her family continued their mission work at Haines until 1886. By then they had realized their dream of a boarding home for Chilkat children.

Chilkat Children's Home, Haines, Alaska, 1886

Annotated Biographical List

Adam — a Chilkat schoolboy; Bessie Ann Frazer's little brother.

Adeline — Chilkat girl who died; daughter of Phillip and Sarah.

Anahootz — a chief at Sitka.

Annie — Chilkat adolescent girl.

Alonzo E. **Austin** — in charge of the mission at Sitka when the Willards arrived in 1881.

Mrs. **Austin** — wife of Alonzo E. Austin.

Miss Linnie **Austin** — school teacher at Sitka in the early 1880s; daughter of Mr. & Mrs. Alonzo Austin.

Mrs. **Beardslee** — wife of Commander Beardslee, who was Commander of the *U.S.S. Jamestown* before Captain Glass, and who, at the suggestion of S. Hall Young, named Muir Glacier after the renowned naturalist John Muir..

John G. **Brady** — First Presbyterian missionary at Sitka, 1878, who resigned this position after a few months in order to go into business with the hope of employing Native men and teaching them industrial skills. He later became Governor of Alaska.

Indian **Charley** (AKA Sitka Charlie) — traveled by dugout canoe with Rev. S.Hall Young and Mr. John Muir in 1879 to explore the Alexander Archipelago north of Fort Wrangell.

Chilkats — subgroup of Tlingit Indians of SE Alaska.

Cla-not — a Chilkat chief; the first of his people to whom Sheldon Jackson promised a missionary for the Chilkats. When the Willard's arrived, he was in line to succeed Chief Don-a-wok, his uncle.

Dr. W. H. R.. **Corlies** — doctor and missionary at Wrangell.

Mrs. **Corlies** — wife of Dr. Corlies.

Mr. **DeGroff** — in charge of the Willard's mail while it was warehoused in or passed through Juneau.

George **Dickinson** — trader and storekeeper for the North-West Trading Company.

Mrs. Sarah **Dickinson** — a Tsimpsian woman; a teacher; the Willard's interpreter; wife of George Dickinson.

William "Billy" **Dickinson** — son of Mrs. Dickinson.

Don-a-wok — a Chilkat chief whose name means "silver eye," a name given him after he had accepted a pair of silver-rimmed glasses from a Russian officer. In 1879, he was among those Chilkats who met with S. Hall Young and John Muir and who selected and turned over to Mr. Young the Portage Bay site which would later become the Haines Mission under the Willards. In 1881 he hosted the Willards during their first visit to the lower villages. He claimed Mr. Willard as his brother. According to Mrs. Willard, "Don-a-wok" was also the name given to Mr. Willard by the Chilkats.

Father William **Duncan** — priest at Port Simpson; founder of the Metlakatla Mission in British Columbia, Canada, and later on Annette Island in Alaska.

Maggie J. **Dunbar** — charter member of the first American church in Alaska at Fort Wrangell. Miss Dunbar was working under the supervison of Mrs. McFarland when the Willards stopped at Wrangell in 1881. She later married Rev. John McFarland.

Esther — the mother of a boy who died and was

buried according to Christian funeral customs; neice of Chief Don-a-wok.

Fanny — orphaned Chilkat schoolgirl whom the Willards took into their home. In time, she became the Willard's interpreter.

Bessie Ann **Frazer** — teenage Chilkat schoolgirl whom the Willards took into their home.

Henry **Glass** — Commander of the USS *Jamestown*.

Miss Clara A. **Gould** — a teacher at Jackson [Hydah].

Mrs. **Haines** — chairwoman of the Women's Executive Committee of the Presbyterian Home Mission Board after whom the Willard's mission site, "Haines," was named.

Mrs. Chilkoot **Jack** — a Sitka lady to whom Mrs. Willard taught sewing.

Sitka **Jack** — Native man whose demands stirred trouble between the tribes.

Dr. Sheldon **Jackson**, D.D. — the first American minister to explore mission possibilities in Southeast Alaska. He became well known and respected as a mission organizer and fund-raiser, and was instrumental in establishing the first American church in Alaska and schools for Natives, one of which was named after him, the Sheldon Jackson Institute (today: Sheldon Jackson College) at Sitka. He was largely responsible for securing funding for and arranging for the construction of the first mission buildings at Haines, and for establishing the first post office there. He traveled throughout the United States on behalf of the Alaska missions and published several papers and books about Alaska. Dr. Jackson became the Alaska Commissioner of Education after Alaska was purchased by the United States.

Moses **Jamestown** — an orphaned Hoonah boy who went to Sitka and under the aid of the commanding officer of the *U.S.S. Jamestown* became a schoolboy there under Mr. Austin's guardianship.

Skookum **Jim** — a Chilkat man.

Mrs. Harry **Kah-dum-jah** — a Chilkat woman to whom Mrs. Willard taught sewing.

Kaht-Lutl — Chilkat chief and medicine man.

Katch-Keel-Ah — a Native child the Willards took in.

Miss **Kellogg** (later Mrs. S. Hall Young) — a teacher in Sitka for six months in 1881 and then wife of Rev. Young in Wrangell.

Rev. Henry **Kendall**, D.D. — Secretary of the Presbyterian Board of Home Missions, who arrived at Fort Wrangell on July 14th, 1879, to explore the potential for further mission work in Southeast Alaska. He and his companions (Dr. A.L. Lindsley, and Dr. Sheldon Jackson) held counsels with the Natives, organized the first American church in Alaska, and made plans for future mission work.

Kittie — a Native girl from Wrangell who stayed with the Willard's throughout the summer of 1881.

Drs. Aurel & Arthur **Krause** — brothers; Doctors of Natural Science from Berlin, Prussia, who spent the spring of 1882 boarding at the cannery near Haines and studying the natural world, the geography of the area, and the Tlingits.

Mrs. C.H. **Langdon** — donated Haines Mission bell.

Lawrence — a boy at the Sitka Home.

Leah — a wife of Phillip.

Indian **Lot** — a Tlingit man from Wrangell who was in 1879 one of the few Native charter members of the first American church in Alaska, and who visited the Willards at Haines in April of 1882.

Captain Edward P. **Lull** — succeeded Captain Glass as commander of the *U.S.S. Jamestown.*

G. W. **Lyons** — missionary at Sitka for one year.

Mrs. **McFarland** — arrived in Fort Wrangell in 1877 to engage in missionary work. She established the McFarland Home and taught Native children.

Rev. John **McFarland** — a layman ordained a missionary. He married Miss Dunbar at Fort Wrangell.

Mark — one of the Willard's first students at Haines.

Miss Elizabeth L. "Bessie" **Matthews** — in Sitka while the Willards were there in 1882. In 1883, she opened a school in Haines.

Captain **Merriman** — of the man-of-war *Adams.*

Minnie — a Chilkat girl.

Mollie — a Chilkat woman; Leah's sister, who Phillip also took into his home.

Nauk-y-stih — the Indian name given to Mrs. Willard by the Chilkats. She understood it to mean *cinnamon bear's head.*

Ned — a Chilkat schoolboy in line to succeed Cla-not and Don-a-wok. He was taken in by the Willards.

Owl — character in Tlingit mythology.

Paul — Chilkat boy in line to succeed Cla-not.

Louis & Tillie **Paul** — Native teachers/missionaries in the upper village who had been educated at the McFarland Home in Fort Wrangell.

Phillip — Chilkat silversmith; husband of Sarah and father of Adeline; later husband of Leah, whose sister Mollie he also took into his home..

Mrs. B.F. **Potter** — a member of the Ladies' Home Mission Society of Schenectady, New York, to whom Mrs. Willard wrote at times.

Miss Kate A. **Rankin** — assistant to Mrs. McFarland of Fort Wrangell.

Raven — the Creator, according to Tlingit beliefs.

Rebecca — a Chilkat woman; mother of Willis; sister-in-law to Chief Don-a-wok.

Sarah — wife of Phillip and mother of Adeline.

Shat-e-ritch — Chilkat chief at Klukwan Village, whose name means "hard to kill." In the late 1860s, soon after the purchase of Alaska by the United States, he had met with U.S. Secretary of State William H. Seward. In 1879, he was among those Chilkats who met with S. Hall Young and John Muir and who selected and turned over to Mr. Young the Portage Bay site which would later become the Haines Mission under the Willards.

Sitkas — subgroup of the Tlingit Indians of SE Alaska.

Snow people — the Chilkat's nickname for the Willards and other white people.

Stickeens — subgroup of the Tlingit Indians of SE Alaska.

Sticks — Native group of interior Alaska with whom the Chilkats annually traded.

Walter B. **Styles** — son-in-law of the Austins; teacher at Hoonah. He worked on construction of the Sheldon Jackson Institute buildings in Sitka. His wife was the youngest daughter of Mr. & Mrs. Alonzo E. Austin.

Lieutenant F.M. **Symonds** — U. S. Navyman serving under Captain Glass on the *U.S.S. Jamestown.*

Tlingit Sawye K-Cotz-e — name given to young Carrie Willard by the Chilkats. The Willards understood it to mean *a mighty city*. They often called young Carrie "Kotzie" thereafer.

Tillie — Chilkat adolescent girl. (not Tillie Paul)

Captain **Vanderbilt** — involved in the October of 1882 skirmish at Kill-is-noo.

Carrie M. **Willard** — wife of Eugene Willard; teacher and founding figure at the first Christian mission at Haines, Alaska.

Eugene **Willard** — husband of Carrie M. Willard; first Christian missionary at Haines, Alaska.

Carrie "Kotzie" **Willard** — daughter of Carrie & Eugene Willard.

Frederick Eugene Austin **Willard** — son of Carrie & Eugene Willard.

Willis — one of the Willards' first students in Haines.

Rev. S. Hall **Young** — Presbyterian missionary at Fort Wrangell; instrumental in organizing the first American church in Alaska. He traveled in 1879 by dugout canoe with Mr. John Muir, naturalist, and a group of Indian men to explore the Alexander Archipelago north of Fort Wrangell. The group negotiated for the Chilkat site that later became the Haines Mission under the Willards.

Mrs. S. Hall **Young** — Charter member of the first American church in Alaska at Fort Wrangell; formerly a teacher in Sitka.

Readings and References

Andrews, C. L., SITKA; THE CHIEF FACTORY OF
THE RUSSIAN AMERICAN COMPANY. (Caldwell,
Idaho: The Caxton Printers, Ltd., 1922)

Cox, J. D., Hon., LETTER OF THE SECRETARY OF
THE INTERIOR [to the 41st Congress). (Ex. Doc.
No. 68.)

Emmons, George Thornton, THE TLINGIT INDIANS,
edited with additions by Frederica deLaguna. (Univ.
of Washington Press, 1991)

Gunther, Erna, DIE TLINKIT-INDIANER. An English
language reprint edition of the original work by
Aurel Krause first published in Jena, Germany, in
1885. (1956)

Jackson, Sheldon, Rev., ALASKA AND MISSIONS ON
THE NORTH PACIFIC COAST. (New York: Dodd,
Mead & Company, 1880)

Muir, John, CRUISE OF THE CORWIN. (New York:
Houghton Mifflin Company, 1917)

Muir, John. TRAVELS IN ALASKA. (Houghton Mifflin
Company, 1915)

Young, S. Hall, ALASKA DAYS WITH JOHN MUIR.
(New York: Fleming H. Revell Company, 1915)

Young, Samuel Hall, HALL YOUNG OF ALASKA.
(New York: Fleming H. Revell Company, 1927)

Index

215